MAHANTONGO VALLEY
HOMESTEADS

OF THE HARTER, EISTER, WIEST, TROUTMAN, WERT, BAUM, AND ROMBERGER FAMILIES,

Jordan Township, Northumberland County, Pennsylvania

STEVE AND JOAN TROUTMAN

an imprint of Sunbury Press, Inc.
Mechanicsburg, PA USA

an imprint of Sunbury Press, Inc.
Mechanicsburg, PA USA

Copyright © 2020 by Steve and Joan Troutman.
Cover Copyright © 2020 by Sunbury Press, Inc.

For information about special discounts for bulk purchases, please contact Sunbury Press Orders Dept. at (855) 338-8359 or orders@sunburypress.com.

To request one of our authors for speaking engagements or book signings, please contact Sunbury Press Publicity Dept. at publicity@sunburypress.com.

FIRST DISTELFINK PRESS EDITION: December 2020

Set in Adobe Garamond | Interior design by Crystal Devine | Cover design by Lawrence Knorr | Edited by Lawrence Knorr.

Publisher's Cataloging-in-Publication Data
Names: Troutman, Steve, author | Troutman, Joan, author.
Title: Mahantongo Valley homesteads of the Harter, Eister, Wiest, Troutman, Wert, Baum, and Romberger families, Jordan Township, Northumberland County, Pennsylvania.
Description: First trade paperback edition. | Mechanicsburg, PA : Distelfink Press, 2020.
Summary: The history of early homesteads in the vicinity of Klingerstown, Pennsylvania, is covered from their purchase from the Penns to present.
Identifiers: ISBN : 1-978-620064-55-9 (softcover).
Subjects: HISTORY / United States / State & Local / Middle Atlantic.

Product of the United States of America
0 1 1 2 3 5 8 13 21 34 55

Continue the Enlightenment!

CONTENTS

Introduction

$\mathcal{G}$eorge M. Troutman and Mary S. Troutman were my grandparents. They lived on the farm, which is the subject of this
writing. For their grandchildren's reference, we all referred to
this farm as "down at Mammy's."

I am the oldest of their grandchildren and therefore was blessed
to have known these grandparents for many years. When I was eleven
years old in 1963, my father and mother decided to build a new house.
The location of this new house was determined by the exceptional view
from the hilltop building site. A large portion of the view from the big
living room windows was of Mammy and Pappy's farmhouse and barn,
and outbuildings, which were surrounded by the farm fields. My parents' house is now the home of my daughter, Valerie; her husband, Tim
Specht; daughters Emma, 10, and Leah, age 7. Franklin, the Mastiff dog,
calls it home, as well.

I lived with my parents until 1975 when Joan and I got married.
During the twelve years I lived at home, my second home was "down at
Mammy's." There was so much to be done there on the farm. Pappy put
me at mowing grass and painting fences. I delighted in helping do the
morning and afternoon feeding of the cattle in the barn. Uncle Bruce
kept the grandsons busy making hay all summer long. It was hot and
dusty, but I liked the work. Mammy liked to cook for the farmhands, so
we enjoyed eating at her table several times a day.

As Mammy and Pappy's grandchildren, we were so accustomed to
being there that we thought of this farm as having been part of our family heritage forever. This was not the case. Pappy's father, Victor, and

two sisters had been born and raised here on this farm. Circumstances, including Victor's mother's death and the death of Victor's two sisters in the prime of their lives, forebode a change in farm ownership. George L. Troutman sold the farm to a good friend and neighbor, Samuel B. Wiest. He operated the farm as a good caretaker until Victor, his son, purchased his birthplace. The family of George Monroe Troutman and Mary Sarah Rabuck became the next residents.

George and Mary lived in Klingerstown soon after their marriage in an apartment building, which stood in the parking lot of the currently shuttered Klingerstown Hardware Store. Here George had started a small garage-type repair business on the first floor of the apartment building. This building later burned to the ground sometime after George and Mary had moved to Jordan Township in the farmhouse that George's father, Victor, had purchased.

George worked for his father, Victor, and then as a partner in the Troutman Brothers' business. He did carpentry work like his father. He also continued doing mechanical repairs of company trucks. After the brothers secured a John Deere dealership, George helped to sell and service farm equipment. He also worked as a meat salesman, going door to door marketing the meats and sausages made in the butcher shop. I recall his red truck with black fenders, which he drove to Trevorton and Shamokin. George also tended the livestock in the big Jordan Township barn, which was usually filled with steers and bulls scheduled for slaughtering in Klingerstown at the Troutman Brothers' butcher shop farm.

George was always interested in local history, especially as it pertained to this own family. In his later years, he delighted in attending public sales to purchase old tools which he refurbished. He eventually built a substantial addition to a chicken house and established The George Troutman Museum of Early American Tools. This collection now remains in the family. As a schoolboy, I helped Pappy as he constructed this museum building. Pappy George was a very good carpenter.

Mary Troutman, fondly called by the name of Mammy, was the prime example of a farm grandmother. She arose early each morning at 5:00 AM to prepare breakfast for her own family and sometimes her grandchildren, as well. All her grandchildren lived nearby and often boarded the school bus stopping here at the farm.

She helped George do the barn work, feeding cattle in the barn. Feeding required hay, chop, and silage. She climbed the silo ladder to throw down the silage, which was then shoveled into a wheelbarrow. It then was pushed into the feed entry to move the cattle feed to the eating trough. The trough was situated below the hay rack feeder. Mammy's chores included overseeing the chicken houses. She fed the chickens as well as gathered the eggs. Eggs were then cleaned and packaged for market.

Laundry was also a chore. I remember her washing machine was in the cellar, and the clothes were carried up a flight of stairs to the outside wash line. In later years she welcomed a much-needed clothes drier.

Cooking meals was an endless series of preparations. Most often, three meals a day were put on the farm table. She was a good cook. Often meals had two meat dishes served for dinner and supper. Her table and chairs were usually filled.

In addition to caring for her own and extended family, Mary often had her mother living in the big farmhouse with her. Sarah Rabuck was widowed a long time and was a welcome hand in the kitchen and household chores. Sarah was a wonderful cook and baker. Sarah was also available as a babysitter for the grandchildren. She loved to play board games and put puzzles together.

Mammy did paint-by-number artwork, which was novel at that time. Her grandchildren now prize these framed pictures.

Mammy and Pappy were always interested in further education. The English dictionary was kept handy on the kitchen counter. They also traveled extensively throughout all the continental United States. George planned his sightseeing trips with a quest for knowledge of Native Americans and early American history. As a widow, Mary accompanied Earl and Marion Troutman to see the ancestral homelands on a trip to Germany. Her Pennsylvania Dutch dialect enabled her to communicate with the people of Germany.

In her later years, Mammy had the foresight to distribute her belongings to her family while still living. All her children and grandchildren

Hay and straw fields surround the homes of George Troutman, Allen Rothermel, and William Shadle, 1950s.

were recipients of this wonderful outpouring of family history and treasures accumulated over a lifetime. By the time of her passing, she had been a widow for many years. There was no public sale necessary. She truly gave all of herself to her family.

There are so many beautiful memories and stories left untold about my grandparents. My uncle Bryant Troutman has preserved some written history about his family. Bryant Anson Troutman and his daughter Lori wrote and published *A Short History of Troutman's Meats* several years ago. The publisher was Mixbook (www.mixbook.com). Copies were made and distributed. Copies are still available.

Bryant Troutman and his daughter Sharon published a further family history in *A Collection of Writings by Mary Sarah Rabuck Troutman, "Mammy."* It also was published by Mixbook. Copies are available. The publisher, Mixbook, will print upon demand by the authors Lori Scott and Sharon Schadle.

On the earliest maps of the area, "Hartters Improvement" is noted as being near the residence of Mary Troutman. (see *Troutman/Trautman*

Mary Troutman (Mammy) at home on the farm.

History Volume 1, pg. 596) There are several springs on this farm. Two are in the hollow northeast of Mary Troutman's house. This hollow was a pioneer home location. Nearby, just south of Mrs. Eugene Erdman's home, is a known homesite. Foundation stones and crockery are evident when plowing. Earl Troutman owned this location for many years and cleared the land of thorns and brush, which had overgrown the abandoned site. This was one of his first bulldozing jobs as a young man. He also closed an old hand-dug well at that time. Earl's mother, Mary Troutman, recalls this location as "The Peelers Patch." There is an old story that *zwei Kinner sind dat vergraawe* (two children are buried there).

It is possible that Johannes Hartter's sons lived at some or all these early homesites.

Mary Troutman lived in an old log house built in 1836. The date is preserved on a log underneath the front shutters. This log house is on land designated "Hartter's Improvement" when the property was warranted, surveyed, and patented by the Harters, as recorded by the Penn Family.

The William Penn Family
Sells Parcels of Land

*T*he Penn Family intended only to sell land after it was purchased from the Native Americans. In 1749 the grandsons of William Penn purchased lands which extended north from the Blue Mountain to the Line Mountain. The Line Mountain is so named as it was the northern boundary of this purchase in 1749. The George and Mary Troutman farmland was within this purchase, which included the Lykens Valley and the Mahantongo Valley.

After the land was purchased, it was available for sale. John Harter Sr. was one of the earliest to view lands in the Mahantongo to purchase. The Penn Family land agents provided **warrants** to prospective landowners. The warrants were an official record that stated the amount of acreage requested and identified the neighboring landowners.

An **improvement** upon the warranted land was required as the next step in the purchase of the land. Perhaps a small dwelling was built, land cleared of trees, or cultivation took place. Johannes Harter Jr., the son of Johannes Harter, is recorded as making an improvement where the George and Mary Troutman house now stands.

After an improvement was made to the warranted land, the next step toward ownership was completing a **survey**. Andreas Harter, son of Johannes Harter, is recorded as surveying the warranted land, which would become the George and Mary Troutman farm.

The Penn Family could sell surveyed lands. A **patent** was issued to the new landowner after payment of the purchase price. Sometimes the patent fee was completed over a long period, perhaps even by the next generation.

Johannes and Maria Harter; their sons, John Jr., Jacob, Andrew, and Mathias; and daughters Anna Maria and Catherine established the first Harter homestead on lands adjoining the George and Mary Troutman farm. This homestead is located on what is lately known as Green Acres Farms. This is now owned by Robert and Lori Scott. The land adjoins the Mahantongo Creek.

The first parcels of land sold in the Mahantongo Valley bordered the creek. The Indian trails and the creek provided the only access into the valley. Johannes and Maria Harter first occupied lands along the creek.

The book *Tulpehocken Trail Traces,* published by Sunbury Press, describes the migration of settlers from Berks County northward into Northumberland County.

The book *The Penns' Manor of Spread Eagle and the Mills of the Upper Mahantongo Valley*, published by Sunbury Press, further describes the lands sold by the Penn Family in the Mahantongo Valley.

Mahantongo Creek Dwellings was painted by artist Dave Kessler in 2020. The scene depicted is on the Harter homestead 3000 years ago. Native Americans lived here.

CHAPTER 1

Johannes Harter Family

An improvement in the wilderness was made here by Johannes Harter Jr.

Harter pioneer dwellings are identified on the following pages, which describe the neighboring landowners to the George and Mary Troutman farm.

Johannes and Anna Maria Hartter – Mahantongo Valley Pioneers

The Hartter Family always interested me because I grew up on the land where this early pioneer family settled. John Hartter warranted two tracts of land in 1774 and dwelled there until 1800 when John and Anna

Maria died within four weeks of each other, having been married 47 years. Most of this land was owned by Earl, Bruce, and Bryant Troutman. (See *Troutman/Trautman Family History Volume 1*, pages 588–596). The Mahantongo Creek generally follows the southern boundary of this land.

As a boy, I often walked the vanishing trace of an old wagon road. The road began in Klingerstown, crossed the creek to Bobby Hoffman's farm, and continued past Bryant and Earl Troutman's. From Earl Troutman's, the road continued west along the creek head to Bruce Troutman's farm. This road followed on the north side of the Mahantongo Creek, crossing many hollows with small streams which descended rapidly down the steep cliff to the Mahantongo Creek below.

I believe this old road to have been an earlier path for the native Indians, traveling from the well-known campsite at Spread Eagle to a smaller campsite in the lowland below where the Hartter log cabin once stood. We know of this ancient Indian dwelling place because of the large number of flint points and pottery fragments found by my grandmother, Mary Troutman. These artifacts were found near the creek, south of Bruce Troutman's home (1995).

As the pioneers followed this Indian path, it became one of the valley's earliest roads. It connected several pioneer dwellings now long gone, evidenced only by springs, hand-dug wells, foundation ruins, and Easter lily flowers, which bloom in early spring. This old road was south of the present-day field road, which passes from Bryant Troutman's to Earl Troutman's to Bruce Troutman's.

Johannes and Anna Maria Harter lived in a small log house, located northwest of the farmhouse Bruce Troutman lives in now. Communication with Mark W. Wiest (February 16, 1995) shows a photograph from 1926, taken at the southwest corner of the old log house, which had several windows and a small porch on the southwest side. In the photograph, William Wiest Jr., Helen and Mark's father, is seated on the chair. He built a new house about fifty feet south of the old house, completed in 1926. As soon as the new home was finished, the old log house was torn down. This farmland borders Mahantongo Creek and Tumbling Run. This would have been a good spot for a grist mill. No doubt, this is why Johannes Hartter chose to patent this land since he was a miller by trade.

The Balsam family was a later generation of residents of this original pioneer home. At this time, the location became known as Balsam's Loch. Mrs. John Williams (Dorthy Strohecker) of Hebe, recalled visiting the Balsam children to play with the neighborhood girls. Dorthy remembered a beautiful spring, partly enclosed, some distance south of the log home. Of the Balsam family, she recalled the father originating from an East European country, perhaps Romania. During World War I, when there were many unemployed men, hobos were common in this area. The Balsam family often gave refuge to these traveling men by leaving a mark on a post at the main road marking their lane as a path to food and shelter. Dorthy recalled the Balsam family was not Pennsylvania German and came from the Shamokin area.

1774 – Harter

The Harter History, by Mary Harter, was privately published in 1964. She lived in Key West, Florida. The following information was taken from correspondence with Bea Leemhuis of Erie.

> Andreas Harter was a miller in Oberdigisheim, Wurttemberg, Germany. This is in the Black Forest area, 35 kilometers from Tubingen, Germany. He married Catherine Zahner, the daughter of Peter Zahner. They had 16 children, only nine of whom reached maturity. They probably emigrated with their family on the ship *Osgood* in 1750. There is an Andreas Herther on that ship. His wife and children under 16 would not have been on the list. They settled in Earl town, Lancaster County. (A John Herter was on the list of the ship *Fane* 1749—perhaps he preceded the rest of his family.) This John Harter and his wife, Maria, are buried in Hebe, at Harter's Cemetery, now named David's Cemetery.
>
> Johannes Harter was born in Oberdigisheim, Wurttemberg, Germany, on December 25, 1725. His occupation was miller and yeoman. On December 22, 1800, he died in Mahanoy Township, Northumberland County and his buried in Hebe.
>
> Johannes married Anna Maria (Witzemann?) in 1753. Anna Maria was born in Germany on April 5, 1726, and died in

Mahanoy Township on November 22, 1800. She is buried with her husband in Harter's Cemetery, now David's Cemetery, Hebe.

Johannes Harter purchased land named Cohesion (C-75-73) as surveyed to him from the Penn Family. This is the land currently owned by the Troutman Brothers, recently occupied by George and Mary Troutman. A portion of this is entitled, "John Herter Jr.'s Improvement." This improvement would be on the site where the house and barn are located.

Land survey C-75-75 was initially warranted to Michael Miller. Johannes and Anna Maria Harter later patented this property. Survey C-75-75 adjoins C-75-73 on the west border. C -75-75 is recalled as the Bruce Troutman farm. Johannes and Anna Maria Harter lived in a small log house located northwest of the farmhouse in which Bruce Troutman lived. Communication with Mark W. Wiest in 1995 shows a photograph from 1926 taken

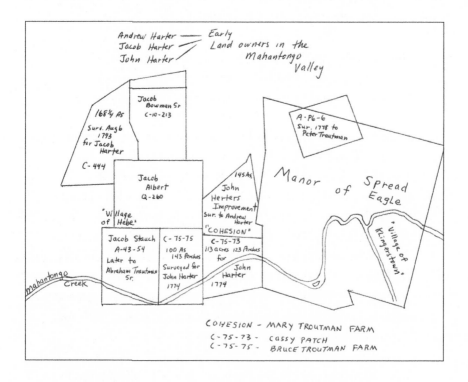

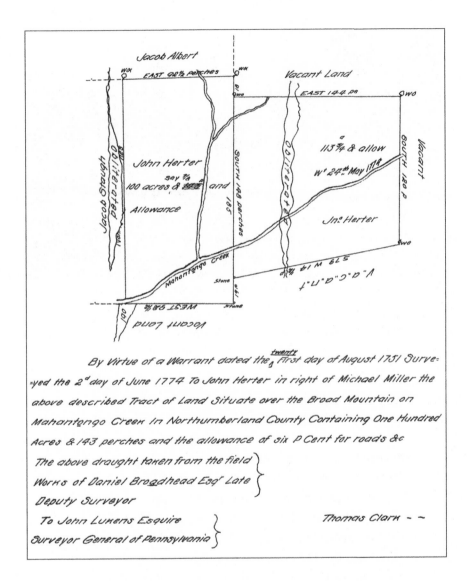

By Virtue of a Warrant dated the twenty first day of August 1751 Surve=
=yed the 2ᵈ day of June 1774 To John Herter in right of Michael Miller the
above described Tract of Land Situate over the Broad Mountain on
Mahantongo Creek In Northumberland County Containing One Hundred
Acres & 143 perches and the allowance of six P Cent for roads &c
The above draught taken from the field
Works of Daniel Broadhead Esqʳ Late
Deputy Surveyor
To John Lukens Esquire   Thomas Clark - ~
Surveyor General of Pennsylvania

at the southwest corner of the old log house, which had several
windows and a small porch on the southwest side. William Wiest
Jr., the father of Mark, built a new house about 50 feet south of
the old house completed in 1926. A soon as the new home was
finished, the old log house was torn down. This farmland borders
Mahantongo Creek and Tumbling Run. This would have been a

First pioneer Harter log cabin, second larger Harter homestead established higher on the hill. This house was later removed, and a barn was built on the house site. The pioneer cabin was removed in 1926 by William Wiest when he built a new residence 50 feet south of the old log house. This new residence is now the farmhouse and residence of Tristan Scott in 2019.

good spot for a grist mill. No doubt this is why Johannes Harter chose to patent this land since he was a miller by trade.

Mark W. Wiest provided a photograph of a large farmhouse constructed north of the homes described in the above paragraph. This large farmhouse was built of logs by later generations of Harter family sons. This house was dismantled and removed, and a large barn was built on the same site. This farm is the current residence of Robert and Lori Scott. A neighbor, William "Toby" Wiest, who resided on the Hebe By-Pass, recalled that some of the logs from this Harter house were transported approximately a mile to be used to construct his own home. No doubt, some of the house timbers were also reused to build the barn.

The following correspondence is between Mark W. Wiest and Steve E. Troutman. It is regarding the first homestead dwelling of John and Maria Harter. The Balsam family later owned this Harter homestead before ownership by William Wiest. William Wiest is the father of Mark.

February 16, 1995

Dear Steve,

I am replying to your letter of February 7, in regard to the Balsam farm.

My family lived on the Balsam farm in 1925 when my father began building the present house there that Bruce Troutman lives in. The new house was built about 50 feet South of the old house. In photo No. 1 left to right are "Jim" Snyder, Bill Rothermel, and my father William Wiest, Jr., beginning construction. In photos Nos 2 and 3, our father, my sister, Helen, and I are at the old porch, which was at the southwest corner of the old house. Picture #4 is the new house completed in 1926. As soon as the house was completed, the old log house was torn down.

We searched through the old pictures, and I do not have a picture of the old house. You are welcome to keep the enclosed photos.

We are in good health, with medication, at our house this winter. Our best regards to you and all of the Troutmans.

Sincerely,

Mark W. Wiest

Former house of Bruce Troutman, now Tristan Scott.

In 1925, Jim Snyder, Bill Rothermel, and William Wiest Jr. constructed a new house.

The newly constructed Wiest house.

William Wiest Jr. married Dora Agnes Troutman. William Wiest Jr., and children, Helen and Mark, pose on the old house's porch. The log house was removed in 1926.

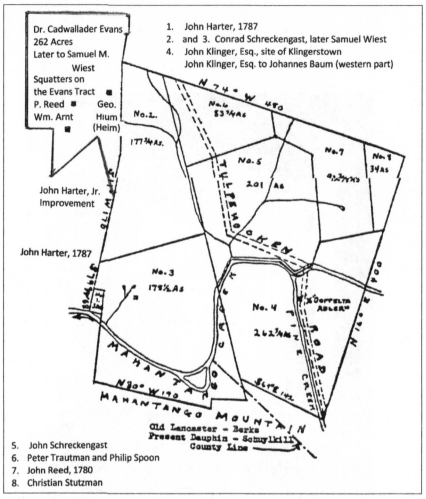

Eight parcels within Spread Eagle Manor. Draft of Spread Eagle Manor in *Early Events in the Susquehanna Valley* by John Carter, p. 150–151.

After the passage of the Divestment Act of 1779, the Manor was re-surveyed and at that time contained 1292 acres. The Penns eventually partitioned Spread Eagle Manor into eight tracts, ranging from 3 to 262 3/4 acreas each.

This draft is mostly the work of Mr. George Wheeler of Philadelphia, a native of Pine Grove. Mr. Wheeler published many articles for historical societies and was associated with the Philadelphia public school system. He was deceased before 1955.

This survey was researched and provided by the Berks County Historical Society. This survey locates John Harter's improvement along the western edge of the Penns' Spread Eagle Manor. This improvement became later known as the George and Mary Troutman farm.

Dr. Cadwallader Evans Tract is not part of Spread Eagle Manor. John Evans was the executor for Dr. Evans. This is presently the Eugene Erdman family farm. John Evans was an absentee landowner, and it is doubtful that he ever lived on his land. Note the squatters on this land, identified as P. Reed, George Hium (Heim?), and William Arnt. There is a legend that the Heim family pioneers are buried in a garden near Klingerstown.

Parcel No. 1, 3A

John Jacob Harter. This could be Jacob (August 09, 1757 – July 12, 1837) from Northumberland County. He married Elizabeth Heim (October 17, 1766 – March 07, 1844) circa 1782-1784. They are buried David's Cemetery, Hebe.

The oldest Harter grave marker is in David's Cemetery, located just outside the Manor boundary. Johannes Hartter, born in Wurttemberg, December 25, 1725, married 47 years, with five children, died December 22, 1800, age 75 years, three days. He married Anna Maria (Witzemann?). Her grave marker is adjacent. It states Anna Maria, born April 5, 1726, in Germany, married 1753, died November 22, 1800, in Mahanoy Township, Northumberland County.

John Harter Jr., born circa 1754, is recorded as dwelling on the land north of his brother Jacob, where the farm of George and Mary Troutman is in Jordan Township, Northumberland County. John's improvement was the first made to this property, which borders the manor on the west side

The Harter family became quite numerous in the Hebe area, where Andrew, Jacob, Mathias, and John were early landowners, having surveys completed by 1774. (See *Trautman-Troutman Family History Volume 1*, page 596, by Steve E. Troutman. See homestead photos on later pages.)

The descendants of Johannes and Maria Harter included six children, many of whom lived on the lands surrounding the George and Mary Troutman farm. One daughter, Catherine Heim, predeceased her parents, so there are only five children listed on Johannes Harter's grave marker.

Parcels No. 2 and No. 3, 177 3/4 A. and 178 1/2 A

Conrad Shreckengaust Parcel No 2 would be the John Rothermel farm now owned by the Eugene Erdman family, and Joe and Ruby Michetti now own the William Rothermel farm.

Benjamin Shreckengaust was the son of Conrad Shreckengaust. Benjamin was born on the John Rothermel Farm north of Joe and Ruby Michetti. Benjamin became a grist mill owner and operator near Red Bank, Clarion County. Benjamin has many descendants.

Parcel No 2 also includes the William and Tim Landis Farm and the Charlie Erdman Farm located on the Tulpehocken Path highway north of Klingerstown. Conrad Schreckengaust has earlier warranted parcels number 2 and 3 but did not patent the land. The Schreckengaust brothers chose to move further westward in Pennsylvania, where unsettled lands were available to purchase.

Benjamin Shreckengaust

It is unknown whether John Harter accompanied his parents to America, or if he came at another time; he did not sign the list. However, this does not mean that he was not on the ship. He may have married in Germany or America. His children were no doubt born in Berks County. On May 16, 1774, John Weber sold 100 acres in Northumberland County to John Harter of Bern Township, a miller. (DB #L page 455, recorded August 11, 1801). Thus, we see that John followed the same occupation as his father, also that this deed was not recorded until after his death. There is a patent to John Harter for 214 acres of land on Mahantongo

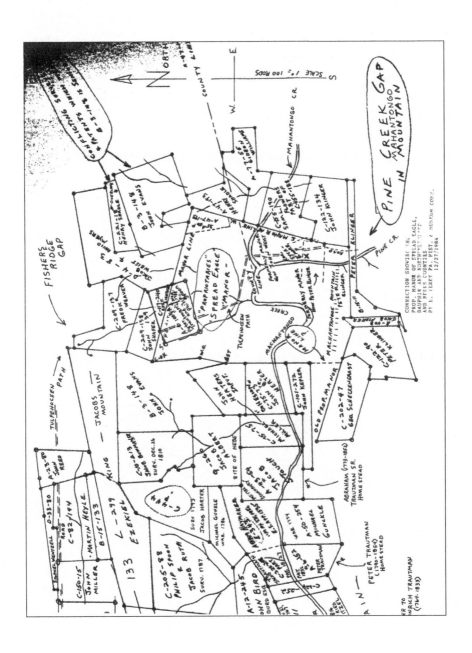

Creek adjoining Jacob Stauch and Jacob Albert surveyed by warrants of May 24, 1774, and one to Michael Miller dated August 21, 1751 (DB #1_page 440, also recorded in 1801). Possibly Michael Miller was the father-in-law of John Harter, or he could have purchased this warrant.

The family of John Harter attended Schwaben Creek or Himmel's Church, Washington Township, Northumberland County, and the records show the family as Lutheran communicants on most of the lists. Mrs. Anna Maria Harter appears much more often than John. There are several baptisms and confirmation of this family in these records. There are no Harter tombstones at Himmel's, and by 1830 the families were attending other churches.

References for the Revolutionary service of John Harter is found in *Pennsylvania Archives, 5th Series, Volume 8*, page 662: 4th Battalion, Northumberland County Militia, muster roll of Captain Benjamin Weiser's Company private #25 John Harter, #21 John Heim (husband of Anna Catharine Harter). This service may be for the son John Harter.

The interesting will of John Harter was made June 18, 1798, and recorded January 6, 1801 (WB #1 page 235). The original will, written in German script, was not in the writing of John Harter. However, he signed both this and the codicil in a very good script.

David's Cemetery, Hebe, Pennsylvania. John and Mary Harter's red sandstone markers are in the front row.

The will of John Harter, June 18, 1798

I, John Harter, in Mahanoy Township in Northumberland
county and state of Pennsylvania, farmer, am at present old and
weak in body but God be thanked in sound sense and memory,
having observed the mortality of mankind I, therefore, make this
my last will and testament hereinafter mentioned.

1st. I commend my soul to the Great Merciful God who gave
me the same, and my body in a Christian like manner to be buried, as for the same it was created, and my worldly goods I divide
as follows after my last debts are paid by my hereinafter named
executors who shall be named hereafter.

2nd. I give and bequeath to my beloved wife, Anna Maria
Harter, the house wherein I at present live, and my sons Andreas
and Mathias Harter shall keep it in good order and repair at
their own expense, and also a cow which she shall choose herself
amongst my cows, and my two sons, Andreas and Mathias,
shall find her good pasture in the summer and keep her in good
provender in the winter. And she shall choose herself another
cow yearly, amongst my son's cows, during her natural life. And
also deliver her yearly and every year twelve bushels good wheat,
six bushels good rye, and also twenty-five pounds good pork,
and twenty-five pounds good beef, and also two gallons of good
honey, and a row of apple trees, she to have the choice, and one
other three near her house and a part in the cabbage garden to
plant something therein and one-half bushel of salt, one half
pound pepper, one pound of ginger, two pounds hogs lard, also
to carry her grain to mill and deliver, to her house a sufficient
quantity of small cut firewood and also five yards flaxen, and five
yards tow linen and calico, one handkerchief and one pound of
wool. All the above mentioned shall be delivered to my beloved
wife, Anna Maria, yearly, and every year by my said sons during
her natural life.

3rd. I give and bequeath also to my beloved wife of my household goods, one bed and bedstead, one blanket and three coverlets, three sheets, three towels, three tablecloths, three bags, one book called the True Christianity, one chest, and the kitchen dresser, and my brass kettle and one iron kettle, and the middle pot, two pewter basins, and one pewter dish, six pewter spoons, and the iron ladle and flesh fork, three pans the porcelain plates, the tea kettle, and the tea crockery. And if she should get sick or confined to her bed, then my said two sons shall give her good attendance or pay 10 pounds for a good attendant so long as she lays sick. And after her decease shall the household good which I bequeathed her, and what is left, shall be equally amongst my six children.

4th. I give and make over to my two youngest sons to wit, Andreas and Mathias Harter, the land and plantation whereon I at present live including all standing in the before mentioned township and county. I say I give and make over to my two sons, Andreas and Mathias Harter, to have and to hold to them, their heirs and assigns forever for which they shall pay the sum of 200 pounds current money of Pennsylvania as hereinafter mentioned.

5th. All my personal property which I have not bequeathed before, my executors, who shall be named hereinafter shall immediately after my decease shall make vendue and the money arising from the same shall within one year after my decease be divided into six equal shares amongst my six children. And the division shall be made by my executors who shall be named hereafter and that what each child has received of me in my lifetime shall be deducted so that to make it equal amongst them. And what each has received is clearly to be seen in a handbook which I made for that purpose. And my eldest son John Harter shall have 10 pounds besides his share of my personal property.

6th. Respecting the two hundred pounds money which my two sons, Andreas and Mathias, are to pay for the before mentioned land, they shall pay to my oldest son, one year after my decease, the sum of sixteen pounds, thirteen shillings, and four pence, and then the second year to my oldest daughter, Anna Maria, Peter Smith1s wife, the same sum as is to be seen by her brother John. And the third year to Jacob Harter the same sum as may be seen by his brother John and the fourth year they shall pay Catherina, John Heim's wife, the same sum of sixteen pounds, thirteen shillings, and four pence and then the following four years to wit, the 5th, 6th, 7th, and eighth year and each heir as they follow one another. The sixth year to Anna Maria the same sum as before mentioned and them the seventh year the same sum as before mentioned and then the eighth year to Catharina, John Heim's wife, the same sum of sixteen pounds, thirteen shillings and four pence current money of Pennsylvania and so each of my children hath his portion.

I appoint and nominate my son Andreas Harter and my son Mathias Harter to be my executors of this my last will and testament, and hereby make null and void all other wills and testament by me make, and I acknowledge this to be my last will and testament and no other. In witness whereof, I have hereunto set my hand and seal the eighteenth day of June one thousand seven hundred and ninety-eight.

Signed, sealed, and publicly   *John Harter*
declared by the above named
John Harter, this to be his
last will and testament in our presence as
witnesses at his request hereunto
subscribed.

Jacob Bauman
Michael Henninger
A true translation to the best of my knowledge and abilities.
Martin Withington.

Jacob Bauman and Michael Henninger were witnesses. Andreas and Mathias were appointed executors. On May 13, 1799, a codicil was added to provide for his grandchildren in case of his daughter's death. George Henninger witnessed this.

After his death, an inventory of his property was made by Jacob Bauman and George Henninger on January 15, 1801. His property included three heads of cattle, part of a calf, two pitchforks, two log chains, iron kettle, grinding stone, nine beehives, seven buckets, five iron pots and a kettle of copper, three beds and bedsteads, four pair of wool pants, two earthen crocks, wooden clock, books, a Bible, knives, forks, cups, dishes, four chairs, two blankets, a quart of beeswax, and two tablecloths—among other things.

Expenses charged to his estate included such items as a gravestone, coffin, translation of will (which was written in German), innkeeper expenses for witnesses when proving the will, ferriages for witnesses on the road to Sunbury to prove the will, costs for weaving and for tanning a hide, and nine shillings for two days work and some tobacco. Each of his heirs received 24 pounds-11 shillings-1 1/6 d. John received an extra ten pounds as his "birthright." The land John Harter owned was divided between Andreas and Mathias, expecting that they would pay 200 pounds to the other heirs.

Johannes and Anna Maria are buried in Hartter's Cemetery (now David's Cemetery) in Hebe. He is said to be the first man buried there, and the cemetery was named in his honor. The tombstones are of red sandstone and are-ornately carved. Similar stones may be found in the Tulpehocken area of Berks County. Anna Maria's stone is no longer legible, but according to gravestone inscriptions, it reads:

In memory of Anna Maria Hartter, wife of Johannes Hartter
Born on April 5, 1726, died on November 22, 1800. Age 74
years, 7 months, 17 days

Tombstones of Johannes and Anna Maria Harter.

Hie Ruhet	Translated:
Johannes Hartter	Here rests
War Gebo. Im Her-	Johannes Hartter
Zogtum, Wurtemberg	Was born in
D 25 Dec. 1725 Im Ehe	The Duchy Wurttemberg
Stand Lebte Er 47 Jahr	December 25, 1725 Lived in
Hinder Lies 5 Kinder	Matrimony 47 Years and
U Starb D December 22. 1800	Left 5 children
75 Jahr 3 Tag	And died December 22. 1800
	Age 75 less 3 days

Regarding the prior picture, the translation was by Ray J. Dieffenbach of Elizabethtown on March 2, 1985, at the 50th wedding anniversary party of his brother, Frank M. Dieffenbach, and wife Reah (Rothermel) Dieffenbach. Note, Johannes Hartter was married 47 years at the time of his death on December 22, 1800, so he would have married in 1753.

The picture of the back of a stone, probably the funeral text of the deceased. I cannot read it, but it says something about Erde and Himmel (Earth and Heaven).

The pictures were taken at David's Cemetery by Steve E. Troutman, sometime in February 1985. (Schuyler C. Brossman, Rehrersburg - May 4, 1985).

Dr. Alfred Kuby of Edenkoben, Germany, translated the reverse as follows: *Nun gute Nacht o Erde /du Himmel sey gegrust /wo ich getrostet werde/mit dem was ewig ist.* (Now I say Good Night to you, Earth, and I greet you, heaven, where I will be comforted by that what is eternal.)

A Harter Birth and Baptism Record

These two married people, Heinrich Herder, and his married house-wife Sarah, born Draudtmann, is a daughter born, the 25th day of

Enlarged view of the center of the Birth and Baptism Record.

A Harter Birth and Baptism Record (courtesy of Ruby Michetti).

September in the year of Our Lord, 1839. This daughter is born in Jackson Township, Northumberland County, in the state of Pennsylvania, in North America, and was given the Holy Baptism name, Lydia Anna, on October 20 in the year 1839 by Reverend Nicholaus Hemping. The baptism sponsors were Johannes Bohner and his wife, Esther.

According to my research, the Harter info comes from a book on the Harter family written by Mary Harter, *The Harter History*. She was a member of a group of genealogists in Ohio. It was privately published in 1964. Beatrice Leemhuis is a Harter Family historian.

Descendants of Andreas Harter

Andreas Harter was born in 1699 in Balingen, Baden-Wurttemberg, Germany. He died before April 12, 1757, in Earl Township, Lancaster County. He was a miller. Andreas married Anna Catherine Zahner, born 1702, in Swartzwaldkreis, Wurttemberg, Germany, on July 25, 1724, in Swartzwaldkreis, Oberdigisheim, Germany. She was the daughter of Peter Zahner. The couple had seventeen children:

1. **Catherine Harter** was born on October 13, 1724, in Oberdigisheim, Germany. She died March 06, 1807, in Lancaster County, Pennsylvania. She was married to Jacob Glasser.

2. **Johannes (John) Harter** was born December 25, 1725, in Oberdigisheim, Wurttemberg, Germany. He died December 22, 1800, in Mahanoy Township, Northumberland County. He was a miller. He was married approximately 47 years to Anna Maria (Witzemann), born April 5, 1726, in Germany. They were married in 1753. She died November 22, 1800, in Mahanoy Township, Northumberland County. The couple was buried at David's Cemetery, Hebe. They were Lutheran and resided in Jackson Township, Northumberland County. They had the following children:

   A. **John Harter** was born circa 1754. He resided in 1802 in Brushcreek Township, Highland County, Ohio. He married Maria Elizabeth circa 1783. They had the following children:

      a. **Peter Harter** was born on September 14, 1783. His baptism sponsors were Peter Albert and wife Regina.

      b. **Elizabeth Harter** was born on January 23, 1785. Her baptism was on August 14, 1785, at Himmel's Church. Her baptism sponsors were Maria Margaret Reid, single. She married Felix Huffman. She died in Ohio.

   c. **Andreas Harter** was born on January 6, 1787. His baptism sponsors were Andreas Harter and Magdalena Rid.

   d. **Jacob Harter** was born on September 6, 1788. His baptism was during October 1788 at Klingers Church. His baptism sponsors were Jacob Stauch and Catherine.

   e. **Anna Barbara Harter** was born on January 18, 1792. Her baptism was in 1792 at Klingers Church. Her baptism sponsors were Barbara Reid, single.

   f. **Mathias Harter** was born circa 1794. His baptism was in 1794 at Klingers Church.

   g. **Leonard Harter** was born circa 1799.

B. **Anna Maria Harter** was born circa 1755 and married Peter Schmidt. They had the following children:

   a. **Johannes Schmidt** was born on March 5, 1775. His baptism sponsors were Johan Harter and Elizabeth Klinger, both single.

   b. **Anna Maria Schmidt** was born on October 2, 1779. On October 7, 1779, her baptism was at Lykens Valley Church, David's Reformed, Killinger, Dauphin County. Her baptism sponsors were Johannes Hoffman and his wife, Anna Maria.

   c. **Jacob Schmidt** was born on November 28, 1788. His baptism was January 19, 1789, at Klingers Church. His baptism sponsors were Jacob Hahn and Magdalena.

C. **Jacob Harter** was born on August 9, 1757. He died July 12, 1837, in Northumberland County, and is buried at David's Cemetery, Hebe. He married Elizabeth Heim, born October 17, 1766, circa 1782 to 1784. They had the following children:

a. **John Jacob Harter** was born on February 3, 1786. His baptism sponsors were Johann Herter and his wife, Maria Elizabeth.

b. **Johannes Harter** (July 24, 1787 – January 17, 1846). His baptism sponsors were Mathais Heim and Magdalena Reid.

c. **Johann Wilhelm Harter** (July 14, 1794 – 1803). His baptism sponsors were John Wilhelm Heim and his wife, Elisabeth.

d. **Mathias Harter** (October 4, 1796 – March 15, 1870). His baptism sponsor was Mathais Herter.

e. **Johann George Harter** was born on September 20, 1798. His baptism sponsors were Jacob Bauman and his wife, Susanna.

f. **Daniel Harter** was born on August 4, 1800. His baptism sponsors were Peter Boly and his wife.

g. **Wilhelm Harter** was born on March 6, 1803. His baptism sponsors were Wilhelm Heim and his wife, Elisabeth.

h. **Magdalena Harter** was born on July 1, 1806.

i. **Samuel Harter** was born on April 23, 1807.

j. **Elizabeth Harter** was born on May 9, 1789. Her baptism sponsors were Andrew Harter and Elizabeth Rissinger.

D. **Anna Catherine Harter** was born circa 1760. She died between May 1799 and December 1800 in Northumberland County. She married John Heim, born 1756, circa 1779. He died in 1824 in Klingerstown. They had the following children:

a. **Mary Catherine Heim** (July 3, 1780 – August 30, 1861). She died in Delaware County, Ohio. She married Frederick Weiser (1776 – May 10, 1800). They lived in Ohio.

b. **Elizabeth Heim** (November 14, 1782 – December 1, 1782). She was baptized at Himmel's Church, Washington Township, Northumberland County. Her baptism sponsor was Elizabeth Heim.

c. **Anna Maria Heim** was born on September 19, 1785. Her baptism sponsors were Andreas Herter and Susannah Pfeiffer, single.

d. **Susannah Heim** was born on October 27, 1787. Her baptism sponsors were Jacob Stauch and wife, Anna Catharina.

e. **Benjamin Heim** (January 23, 1789 – February 14, 1860). He died in Red Cross. He married Magdalena.

f. **Mary M. Heim** (June 15, 1790 – January 18, 1877). She died in Ralpho Township. She married John Swank.

g. **Andreas Heim** was born on March 13, 1792. He was baptized on May 16, 1792, at Klingers Church.

h. **Maria Salome Heim** was born on November 8, 1796. Her baptism sponsors were Mathais Heim and his wife, Magdalena Heim.

E. **Andreas Harter** was born circa 1765. He married Magdalene (Anna Maria) after 1785. The couple had the following children:

a. **Catharina Harter** was born on July 1, 1792. She was baptized in 1792 at Klingers Church.

b. **Johannes Harter** was born in 1793.

c. **Benjamin Harter** was born on June 1, 1802.

d. **Maria Magdalena Harter** was born on June 11, 1804. Her baptism sponsors were Samuel Bauman and Magdalena Esterlein, both single.

e. **Isaac Harter** was born on February 15, 1806. He was baptized in 1806 at Klingers Church.

F. **Mathias Harter** was born circa 1775 in Northumberland County. He died between 1820 and 1829 in Northumberland County. He resided in Upper Mahanoy Township, Northumberland County. Benjamin and Esther may be the names of unknown children. He married Elizabeth Bauman, born circa 1782, circa 1798, most likely in Northumberland County. She died after 1829 in Northumberland County. Her baptism sponsor was Mathais Harter. She is probably buried in Harter's Cemetery, Hebe. The couple had the following children:

a. Boy born before 1800.

b. Girl born between 1800 and 1804.

c. **Susanna Harter** was born on May 1, 1803. Her baptism sponsors were Jacob Bauman and his wife, Susanna.

d. Girl born between 1804 and 1810.

e. **Johannes Harter** was born circa April 1805.

f. **Catherine Harter** was born on January 27, 1809.

g. Girl born between 1810 and 1820.

h. Girl born between 1810 and 1820.

i. **Sarah Harter** was born on April 7, 1811.

j. **Henry Harter** was born April 5, 1816, in Northumberland County. He died after 1850 in Northumberland County. He was baptized on July 7, 1816, at Klingers Church. His baptism sponsors were Samuel Geise and wife Hannah. He was Lutheran. He married Salome Trautman, born June 30, 1816, in Northumberland County, circa 1837. She died on April 15, 1848, in Northumberland County. She is buried at David's Cemetery, Hebe. Henry then married Susannah Miller, born 1818, before 1850.

k. **Elias Harter** was born on August 7, 1819.

3. **Johann George Harter** was born circa 1729 in Oberdigisheim, Germany. He died in Franklin County, Virginia. He married Anna Eva Mikesell, born April 14, 1730, in 1753 at St. Peter's Lutheran Church. They had the following children:

A. **Christian Harter** was born circa 1754 in Bedford County. He died in 1825 in Lanier Township, Preble County, Ohio. He married Maria Elizabeth Eller, born in Frederick County, Maryland, in 1775 in Bedford County. She died in 1815 in Ohio. They had the following children:
   a. **Susanna Harter**
   b. **Phoebe Harter**
   c. **John Harter**
   d. **Katherine Harter**

B. **George Harter** was born in 1755 in Bedford County. He died March 23, 1843, in Lanier Township, Ohio, and is buried in Holderman Cemetery. He married Mary Ketterman in 1776.

C. **Christina Harter** was born circa 1757. She married Adam Kruger in 1777.

D. **Catherine Harter** married Christopher Meyer.

E. **Conrad Harter** was born in 1762 in Bedford County. He died in 1823 in Ohio. He married Elizabeth Hoffert.

F. **Dorothea Harter** was born in 1766. She married Zachariah Allbaugh.

G. **Elizabeth Harter**.

H. **Maria Harter** may have married Allbach.

I. **Frantz Harter** was born in 1759 in Bedford County. He died in 1832 in Darke County, Ohio. He married first Susan Ketterman circa 1780. He married Catherine Kurtz in 1787.

J. **Jacob Harter** was born in 1760 in Bedford County. He died in December 1824 in Hagerstown, Maryland. He married Magdalena in 1785.

K. **Adam Harter** was born in 1768 in Bedford County. He married Margaret Macdonald.

4. **Adam Harter** was born on October 4, 1729, in Oberdigisheim, Germany, and died before 1740.

5. **Anna Maria Harter** was born on December 26, 1730, in Oberdigisheim, Germany.

6. **Anna Harter** was born on January 13, 1733/34.

7. **Dorothea Harter** was born on February 14, 1734/35, in Oberdigisheim, Germany.

8. **Barbara Harter** was born on June 9, 1736.

9. **Matthias Harter** was born on June 5, 1737, in Oberdigisheim, Germany. He died in Dauphin County. He married Schuler.

10. **Andreas Harter** was born on February 8, 1738/39, in Oberdigisheim, Germany. He died November 14, 1814, in Ephrata, Lancaster County, and is buried there. He married Anna Barbara Kramer.

11. **Simon Harter** was born on October 28, 1740.

12. **John Peter Harter** was born on September 9, 1742. He died before 1743.

13. **Peter Harter** was born on November 9, 1743.

14. **Jacob Harter** was born May 16, 1745, in Oberdigisheim, Germany. He died May 7, 1812, and is buried in Barnwell County, South Carolina.

1790 CENSUS

John Herter	3	-	1
John Herter, Jr	1	4	2
Jacob Herter	1	2	2

1800 CENSUS

John Harter	Nor 815	40010-20010-00
John Herter	Nor 706	23011-21001-00
Mathias Herter	Nor 706	10001-00100-00
		(May be an error in age)
Jacob Herter	Nor 706	32010-01010-00
Andrew Herter	Nor 706	30010-20010-00

John Harter and Anna Maria had six children. His daughter, Catherine, predeceased him, so his tombstone mentions only five children. In 1774 John Harter warranted, surveyed, and patented several tracts of land in the Hebe area of southern Northumberland County, neighboring the Manor of Spread Eagle. He was on a list of taxables in Mahanoy Township in 1778. In 1790 his Sons Andreas and Mathias still lived with their parents, but by 1800 they had started their own families. On June 18, 1798, he wrote a will.

1800 CENSUS

Mathias Herter	Nor 706	10001-00100-00
		(Mathias's age may be an error)

1820 CENSUS

Mathias Hatar (Harter)

Males:		Females:	
2 under 10		3 under 10	
1 between 10 and 16		2 between 10 and 16	
1 16-26		2 16-26	
1 over 45		1 over 45	

Mathias and his brother Andreas were executors of their father's will, and they received his farm for which they paid other heirs 200 pounds. He lived in Upper Mahanoy Township, Northumberland County. The will of Jacob Bauman proved in 1829 mentions his daughter, Elizabeth, widow of Mathias Harter.

Johannes Hartter Homestead. William Wiest Jr. seated, Helen and Mark Weist with their doggies.

Harter Family Millstone

The early history of the Harter family in lower Northumberland County includes their occupation as millers. An artifact has been located confirming this vocation. A millstone has been found between Klingerstown and Hebe on land occupied by Harter family descendants. See the enclosed photos. The stone is very heavy and appears to be the bedstone of a pair of millstones. A typical set of millstones found within a grist mill usually includes a stationary bed stone and a runner stone, which turns on top of the bed stone. The Harter stone is not typical of grist millstones where the bed stone has many grooves carved on its face to carry the ground flour or meal to the edge of the stone.

The Harter mill bedstone is concave or dish-shaped, with a side notch cut into the stone's raised edge. This v-shaped notch would facilitate the exit of the milled material as the smaller diameter runner stone was turning on top of the bed stone, within the bed stone.

The Harter family did own land bordering Mahantongo Creek, which could have accommodated a grist mill location. There is no evidence or tradition of this Harter family having established a water-powered grist mill on Mahantongo Creek.

The earliest pioneers grew flax to make linen cloth. The seeds produced the linseed oil used for many purposes. Linseed oil was burned with a wick in a lamp to produce light. Perhaps this Harter millstone was used for crushing flax seeds to produce linseed oil. It is possible that animal power rotated the runner stone.

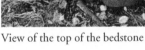

View of the top of the bedstone   View of edge

CHAPTER 2

John S. Eister Family

John S. Eister built the log house in 1836 and the barn in 1840.

The John Eister Family

In October of 2018, I had a conversation with Arlen Lenker of Northumberland. He had stopped by the Lewisburg Farmer's Market at the Troutman Brothers meat stand. He told me that he had an elderly relative, Dr. Donald Eister, who did family research. I asked Arlen to identify the man John Eister named in the *Northumberland County History*, by Floyd. John Eister built the log house on the George and Mary Troutman farm in Jordan Township, Northumberland County, Pennsylvania.

Arlen communicated with Dr. Donald Eister. He identified John Eister as married to Elizabeth Harter. When I heard of this marriage, I knew it was the right John Eister. Earlier research of this property identified it as Harter land. In fact, the Harter's were the first to improve this land and the first to purchase it from the Penn Family.

With this identification of John and Elizabeth Harter Eister, I determined to write a historical account of the many people associated with this farm. The Harter family is one of the earliest to settle in this part of the Mahantongo Valley, now Jordan Township, Northumberland County, Pennsylvania. A historical record of this family has been published in a book entitled *The Penns' Manor of Spread Eagle and the Mills of the Mahantongo Valley* by Steve E. Troutman.

The following pages are reprinted from the book named above, as well as other previous published Eister family histories.

GEORGE L. TROUTMAN, son of John, was born June 21, 1858. He was reared to farm life, and worked for his parents until he attained his majority, after which he began farming on his own account in Upper Paxton township, Dauphin county, where he was a tenant for a few years. In 1881 he came to his present home in Jordan township, a 120-acre farm located on the road between Hebe and Klingerstown, formerly the homestead of John Eister, who built the present barn in 1840 and the house in 1836. Samuel Wiest bought the property from Mr. Eister for his son Jacob, who occupied it for thirty-five years, since when it has been in Mr. Troutman's possession. It has long been regarded as one of the most valuable farms in the valley, its successive owners having taken considerable pride in keeping it up, and it has not deteriorated under Mr. Troutman's management. He is one of the industrious and thrifty farmers of his section.

On Dec. 8, 1878, Mr. Troutman married Mary Wert, daughter of William and Catharine (Riegel) Wert, and they have three children: Alice A., who married John Romberger and lives on the homestead (they have one son, Ralph T.); Victor, of Klingerstown, Pa., married to Sallie B., daughter of Tobias Wiest; and Dora A., who married William B. Wiest, Jr., and is now living in Alberta, Canada, where they settled on a homestead of their own and have prospered.

Mr. Troutman and his family have been identified with the Troutman United Evangelical Church, of which his father was the founder. He is a Republican in political sentiment.

Genealogical and Biographical Annals of Northumberland County, Pennsylvania, by J.L Floyd and Co., 1911, p. 736.

Harter-Eyster Family Connection

Elizabeth Harter married John S. Eyster. This marriage record provided the impetus for the compilation of this material. When I first learned of this marriage, I got goosebumps. Arlen Lenker told me of this connection at the Lewisburg Farmers Market. I knew at that moment this was the missing link between the Harters and the Eysters.

The following information is courtesy of Arlen Lenker of Northumberland, April 25, 2018. Arlen spoke with Dr. Eister regarding Eister family history and any possible connection to the George and Mary Troutman farm in Jordan Township, Northumberland County.

Donald Eister, MD, was a "baby" doctor from Sunbury. He is 97 years old and lives in Williamsport. His son Ronald Eister is also a doctor in Williamsport. Donald Eister, MD, said that there are two John S. Eisters that could have built the log house on the George and Mary Troutman farm:

John S. Eister (October 17, 1786–May 9, 1853) married Elizabeth Harter (May 19, 1789–June 22, 1871). This John is the brother of Abraham Eister.

John S. Eister (January 9, 1826–May 4, 1881) married Caroline Eisenhart, January 27, 1829. This John was the son of Abraham Eister.

Dr. Donald Eister and Steve E. Troutman agree that John S. Eister married to Elizabeth Harter is the log house's builder. Elizabeth Harter was the daughter of Jacob Harter (August 9, 1757–July 12, 1837) and Elizabeth Heim, born October 17, 1766. She was married circa 1782-1784. Both Elizabeth and Jacob Harter are buried in David's Cemetery, Hebe. Jacob and Elizabeth Harter resided on land surveyed 1793 (C-40), located north of the Hebe Church. The township road divides the surveyed land. In his *Troutman Family History*, Ralph Romberger recorded that John Eister built the log house in 1836 and the barn in 1840.

Troy and Audra Eyster are associated with the Snyder-Eyster Insurance Agency in Herndon. Troy's father, David, is an Eyster family historian. An interview with this Eyster family proved to be a great learning experience as I began my research on the Eyster family. Audra had a picture of

John S. Eyster's gravestone on her cell phone, which she showed to me at the Pillow Bicentennial Celebration in 2018.

1836 – Harter to Eyster

The Eister Family History, by Donald H. Eister

John Jacob Aister, born in the state of Wurttemberg, obviously read the "Brief Account" by William Penn, who, in 1681, came into the possession of the next to the last of the thirteen British colonies to be chartered. This picture of opportunity and experiencing religious oppression by the German Princes and the devastation and destruction by local and foreign armies raging war back and forth over their land were the reasons for John Jacob and his family's emigration to the New World. They endured the hardships of pioneer life and thrived and became prosperous.

Seven successive generations made their living from the soil. The early ancestors lived in German colonies and spoke German and lived a simple life. They witnessed the historical events that led to the birth of our nation.

No way could John Jacob Aister (1665–1745) have foreseen that in nine generations, the family farm would disappear, and scientific achievements would land a man on the moon, and the development of all the dramatic changes contributing to our way of life.

Each of us is a descendant with two parents, four grandparents, eight great grandparents, and so on, the numbers in each preceding generation being doubled. Following the doubling process back nine generations to the era of John Jacob Aister and Catherine, it will give each of the children of W. Howard Eister, MD, and Amelia Kublic 256 direct ancestors. All of them were key players in our existence! The number of direct ancestors continues to mount:

> Tenth generation (our children): 512
> Eleventh generation (our grandchildren): 1024
> Twelfth generation (our great-grandchildren): 2048

Considering all the branches of the Eister family tree back to John Jacob Aister and Catherine, the only way to determine the total number of descendants would be by the census. In most families, every couple of generations, someone comes along and records their family history. Descendants might wonder, "who gathered together this information?" Dad and Mother were my early sources. They knew about Nathan and Abraham.

When I was in my early twenties, I heard that cousin Allen had traced the family tree, and I collected his information, which was not complete.

After I came back to Sunbury in 1950 to start the practice of medicine, I started making notes. In 1954 an Eyster family from the Herndon area came to my office with sick children. I was surprised to find out that they knew me to be related and had records. I was able to copy everything they had, and it was a significant find:

JOHN JACOB AISTER (1665 – May 31, 1745) married Catherine and had children:

1. **Magdalen Maria Oyster**, born on December 20, 1694, married Bernard Kepner.
2. **Anna Maria Oyster** died in 1778, married May 15, 1718, Christopher Slagle (Schagle).
3. **Rosina Oyster** married John Shimel.
4. **John Georg Oyster** (1706–1789) married Catherine Arentz (2nd wife).
5. **Christian Oyster** (1710–1747) married in 1732 Margaret Schmeiser (Smyser).

John Jacob Aister, the Eister pioneer to America, was born in 1665 near Stuttgart, Wurttemberg, Germany. He was part of that heavy wave of German immigration, which started in 1683—fleeing from oppression to a land of promise and hope and religious tolerance. By hard experience, sturdy self-reliance, and energy, he was one of the pioneers who adapted or died.

In the death records of the New Hanover Lutheran Church, his name is recorded as Jacob Aister. Further on in the same alphabetic listing, it is recorded again with an umlauted ü: Jacob Aüster. The original German spelling was likely Johannes Jacob Aüster before it was anglicized to John Aister. The following generation spelled the surname Oyster. Subsequently, it was spelled Eyster and then Eister. All three spellings are used today. Aüster is the German word for Oyster.

John Jacob was 16 years of age in 1681 when William Penn was given the Proprietary Grant to the territory of Pennsylvania by the King of England. Penn published in 1682 a pamphlet—*A Brief Account of the Province of Pennsylvania*—to attract colonists. He offered liberal terms, assuring all that they could obtain land, establish thrifty homes, and live in justice and equality with their neighbors. No Christian would suffer from religious discrimination. In civil affairs, the laws would rule, and the people would be a party to the laws. This pamphlet was widely distributed in Germany and other countries.

John Jacob Aister was 18 years old in 1683 when the first group of Germans under the leadership of Reverend Francis Pastorius emigrated to Pennsylvania aboard the ship *Concord*. The first Germans to come to America, as colonists in Pennsylvania, were, as a rule, well to do. Nearly all of them at the beginning of that mighty exodus had sufficient means to pay all the charges in going down the Rhine to the sea, and enough besides to meet the expenses for carrying them across the ocean, and yet have some left when they arrived to pay for part or all the lands they took up.

JOHN GEORG OYSTER (1706–1789) married, second, Catherine Arentz and had children:
1. **Elisabeth Catherina Oyster** (December 23, 1730–January 14, 1812) married in 1747 Johannes Yoder (1718–1812).
2. **Georg Oyster** (1732–1795) married on March 13, 1759, Hannah Moyer.
3. **Samuel Oyster** (1734–1767) married Margaret.
4. **Jacob Oyster** (1736–1780) married Magdalena Burkhouse who died 1780.
5. **Barbara Hannah Oyster** born in 1741 married on April 14, 1761, Peter Keplinger.

6. **Daniel Oyster** (August 18, 1743 – September 13, 1798) married in 1770 Elisabeth Reif (May 18, 1742 – August 21, 1830).
7. **Magdalena Susanna Oyster** born on July 30, 1745, married in 1767 Richard Adams.
8. **Maria Margaretha Oyster** (May 5, 1753 – December 23, 1833) married in 1773 Daniel Yoder (April 22, 1748 – August 21, 1820).

John Georg Oyster was born in 1706. At age eleven, he arrived in America with his parents. He must have understood the political and social unrest in Germany and that the new land was a land of promise and hope. His signature, and that of his brother Christian, is found on the Petition of the New Hanover settlers who are asking for protection from the Indians in 1728. These signatures are written as John Aister and Christian Aigs.

John Georg, age 22, was likely living in the New Hanover area and probably married at that time, but the name of his first wife, to whom he had his children, is unknown. The marriage date is inferred from the date of birth of his oldest daughter in 1730.

He early acquired land, purchasing in 1734 200 acres in Oley Township, Berks County (then Philadelphia County). This land was entirely paid for by 1739, in which year he was naturalized, signing his name as John Aigster. This land became the family homestead.

Land records in Harrisburg show that he had other tracts:

1744: 100 acres in Philadelphia County
1748: 50 acres in Lancaster County
1749: Another 25 acres in Philadelphia County
1756: 50 acres in Roxboro, Philadelphia County
1772 & 1774: He bought considerable tracts in Cumberland County

JACOB OYSTER/EYSTER (1736–1780) married Magdalene Burk-house who died in 1780. They had children:

1. **Jacob Eister** (February 27, 1752 – June 28, 1827) married Phillppina Kump (November 2, 1758 – September 19, 1848).
2. Daughter.
3. **Abraham Eyster** (1775–1864) married Maria Keisicher (1790–1865).
4. **George Eyster** (November 15, 1777 – February 24, 1846) married Elizabeth Keisicker (1778–1856).

Chronology of events in Jacob's life:

1752, age 16   The birth of his son Jacob (1752–1827).

1756, age 20   The onset of the French and Indian War. The thirteen British colonies had a population of 1,500,000. The French population was estimated at 100,000.

1761, age 25   In about 1761, Jacob left Oley, where he was born, and moved his family to Abbottstown, York County, where relatives were living. His brother Daniel Oyster and his aunt Mary Eyster, wife of Christopher Slagle, lived a little southwest of Abbottstown. During the Revolutionary War, Jacob was a Captain, as was his older brother Daniel and had responsibility for logistics and moving wagons.

1763, age 27   The peace treaty was signed. The French lost Canada and the American Midwest.

1764-1767,   Great Britain started tightening administrative controls
age 28 to 31   over the colonies . . . taxation without representation. The Sugar Act, Stamp Act, and Townshend Act.

1770, age 34   The Boston Massacre.

1773, age 37   The Boston Tea Party.

1775, age 39   The birth of second son, Abraham (1775–1864). There was an interval of 23 years between the birth of first, Jacob, and second son, Abraham.

1776, age 40   The Declaration of Independence was signed.

1777, age 41   Birth of third son, George (1777–1846).

1780, age 44   His wife Magdalene died. Jacob (1736–1780) left his 28-year-old son Jacob (1752–1827), a hatter, and his daughter in Abbottstown and took his two younger children Abraham, aged five, and George, aged three, to relatives in Adamstown, Lancaster County. He left for Virginia to buy a farm (just as many Pennsylvania Germans were doing) and was never heard from again. It had been rumored that a man was murdered on the Baltimore Road for the money he was carrying, and his family supposed him to be the murdered man. Relatives raised the children.

JACOB EISTER (February 27, 1752–June 28, 1827), according to *Berks County Marriages 1730-1800*, married Philippina Gump (November 2, 1758–September 19, 1848) on December 27, 1783. Jacob and his new wife were the first Eisters to settle in the Upper Mahanoy Township, Northumberland County, circa 1788. Both are presumed members of Himmel's Church, and both are buried there as attested by Himmel's Cemetery records and copies of the same on file with the Northumberland County Historical Society. We also note the spelling change from Oyster to Eister on the marriage listing and the cemetery records. They had children:

1. **Magdalena Eister** (February 27, 1778–October 12, 1846) married J. Michael Reitz (August 12, 1785–July 28, 1874).
2. **Michael Eister** (February 27, 1784–November 7, 1842) married Anna Barbara Haupt (February 14, 1790–January 26, 1864).

3. **John S. Eister** (October 27, 1786–May 9, 1853) was buried at Snydertown Cemetery. He married Elizabeth Harter/ Harter (May 19, 1789–June 22, 1871).

4. **Daniel Eister** (July 2, 1789–May 12, 1854) was buried Himmel's Cemetery. He married Elizabeth Kembel (July 2, 1796–February 26, 1854).

5. **Abraham Eister** (October 15, 1790–August 16, 1846) married Maria Christiana Stepp (November 12, 1799– September 16, 1842), the daughter of Sebastian Stepp, on March 20, 1819. He then married Catharine Tschopp? circa 1842 to 1846.

6. **George Eister** (born on August 8, 1796) married Margaretha.

7. **Samuel Eister** was buried at Himmel's Cemetery. He married Elizabeth (November 3, 1803–December 6, 1843).

8. **Hannah Eister** (February 10, 1798–April 20, 1866) married Mathias Harter (October 4, 1796–March 15, 1870.)

9. **Sarah Eister** (born on October 22, 1799).

10. **Leah Eister** (born on March 2, 1801) married Solomon Kembel.

11. **Peter Eister** (also born on March 2, 1801).

Jacob was 26 years old, and Phillippina (who lived in Maiden Creek) was 20 years when their first child was born on February 27, 1778. In the biographical sketch of David G. Eyster, *History of Cumberland and Adams Counties, Pennsylvania*, 1886, page 467, it is stated that in 1780 at 28 years of age, Jacob Eister was a hatter. In 1780 when his mother died, his father left to go to Virginia to buy a farm and disappeared, and it was supposed that he was murdered on the Baltimore Road. Jacob and his sister were left at Abbottstown, and his two brothers Abraham, aged five, and George, aged three, were left with relatives at Adamstown.

In a span of 25 years, eleven children were born to Jacob and Philippina. Seven sons and four daughters. These names are listed as his heirs in deed book W, pages 279 and 390. All their names are listed as Oyster, and that they lived in Upper Mahanoy Township, Northumberland County, except for George Eister. He lived in Schuylkill County. At age 44, Jacob's name first appears in the records of Himmel's Church on August 8, 1796, when son George was born. This likely dates his arrival in Upper Mahanoy Township, Northumberland County.

The following land transactions are recorded in the Northumberland County deed books:

- *Book V page 57 5/10/1820:* Jacob Oyster deeded to his son Michael Oyster 108 acres and 22 perches in Upper Mahoney Township for 66 pounds, thirteen shillings fourpence in gold or silver money.
- *Book W page 279 2/7/1828:* Release of heirs of Jacob Oyster to Daniel Oyster, two parcels of land in Upper Mahoney Township. Forty acres and 54 perches and 112 acres and 34 perches. The total sum was $692.97.
- *Book W page 390 2/7/1828:* Release of heirs of Jacob Oyster to George oyster 146 acres and 123¾ perches In Upper Mahanoy Township for the sum of $1,107.03.

Jacob died in May 1827. Letters of administration are recorded in Will book no 3, page 110:

Jacob Oyster, deceased

Be it remembered that on May 12 in the year of our Lord one thousand eight hundred and twenty-seven, Letters of Administration in due and common form of law were granted to John Oyster and Michael Reitz upon the estate of Jacob Oyster late of Upper Mahoney Township, Northumberland County Deceased (the widow having previously renounced) who entered into Bond with Philip Heterick and Denial Gonsert in the sum of Two thousand dollars. Samuel P. Packer, Register

"Feeding the Cows in Winter." Illustration from *Glenson's Fictional*, Boston, February 4, 1854.

Evangelical Lutheran and Reformed Church (now Himmel's Church), Washington Township, Northumberland County, one-half mile east of Rebuck. Founded in 1773.

Himmel's Church Cemetery. Jacob Eister's tombstone is second from the tree.

 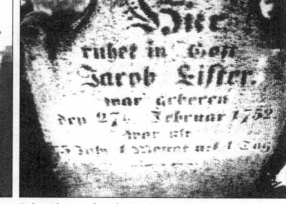

Tombstone of Jacob Eister   Enlarged view of Jacob Eister's tombstone

German translation: We would say:

Here   Here

Rests in God   rest in God

Jacob Eister   Jacob Eister

was born   born on

February 27, 1752   February 27, 1752

was old   lived to be (or- his age was)

75 years 1 month 14 day   75 years 1 Month and 14 Days

Inscription that was on Phillippine Eister's tombstone: In memory of Phillippine, a born Kump, the wife of Jacob Eister, born November 2, 1758, died September 19, 1846. Aged 89 years, 9 months, 17 days.

The grave is now unmarked.

John and Elizabeth Eister Move to Snydertown

In late October 2018, Joan and I traveled to Snydertown to search for the grave markers of John and Elizabeth Eyster. We traveled from Sunbury east on Snydertown Road. St. John's Cemetery is located approximately one mile west of Snydertown on the south side of Snydertown Road. Arlen Lenker recalls a church building on the north side of the highway, which has been removed. Conversations with residents of the community of Snydertown were very fruitful. An old Eyster residence was identified. See the enclosed photo. This home is in Snydertown between the Lutheran church and the railroad tracks at the south edge of town. This Lutheran church, near the town square, is now a community center.

St. John's Cemetery is in fair condition with a new sign. Many of the grave markers need to be straightened, but the grass is being mowed. If John and Elizabeth lived near the Lutheran church in Snydertown, I would guess they attended that church congregation associated with this cemetery. We found the grave markers of John and Elizabeth quite easily. The tall markers stand straight, in good condition, in the center of the cemetery. They are not far from the road.

Why did John S. Eyster and Elizabeth (Harter) Eyster move from rural Jordan Township to Snydertown? John had built a large log house in 1836 and a large barn in 1840 in Jordan Township. John was born in 1786, making him 54 years old at the completion of the barn building. Perhaps he had planned to sell the improved farm for retirement income. However, we need to remember that his wife Elizabeth Harter

John and Elizabeth Eister lived here at 115 Main Street, Snydertown.

St. John's Cemetery, Snydertrown Road, John and Elizabeth Eister are buried here.

had connections to the land where John built the log house and barn. The Harters first occupied this land after purchasing it from the Penn Family. The Harters were the first to improve the land. I believe there was an earlier dwelling here before John and Elizabeth built their log house in 1836. John Harter's improvement is shown here on an early warrant map. There must have been a small log cabin dwelling at the time of the first settlement.

Several years ago, a ditch was dug between the present drilled water well near the farmhouse and the barn. The ditch diggers here uncovered broken red ware style pottery and other china fragments where Mary Troutman's garden used to be located. It is possible this was the location of the earliest cabin that John Harter Jr. lived in. There is a hand-dug well in front of the 1836 log house, which is now covered by the cement walkway. This hand-dug well would have been close to the proposed earlier cabin site. I think the Harters dug this well. There is adequate water supply nearby in a small stream fed by springs close to the house. These springs would have served the earliest residents of any pioneer dwelling.

Another hand-dug well was located south of the 1836 log house on the south side of Klingerstown Road. This well served a small tenant house which stood south of the highway. I remember this well covered by a cement slab close by the road. This well could have been dug by the Harters and may mark a possible pioneer cabin site. The tenant house which stood here, called the little red house, was not the pioneer cabin. See the pictures enclosed.

Elizabeth Harter was born in 1789. Her brother, Mathias, was born in 1796. Mathias Harter married Hannah Eister. Hannah was born in 1798. John and Hannah were brother and sister. Mathias and Hannah lived nearby, north of the location where the Hebe Bypass and Klingerstown Road intersect. So, we have intermarriage of two siblings within the same two families, who resided as neighbors. This concept of dwelling near other family members would seem to make it difficult to move away from the local area. But John and Elizabeth did indeed move from the country to the town. Many years ago, this was common, as the farm work became too much for the older folk to handle.

The Troutman stone house in Spain, near Hebe, where Elizabeth Troutman was born. Elizabeth (1825–1881) married Jacob K. Wiest (1826–1878).

CHAPTER 3

Jacob K. Wiest Family History

The Wiests built some farm outbuildings.

The Wiest family history, which follows, represents the interest and research of many earlier historians. Some are named here, but the list is not
all-inclusive.

Sally Wiest Troutman
George and Mary (Rabuck) Troutman
Earl and Marion (Romberger) Troutman
Ralph and Carrie Romberger, Dr. John A. Romberger
Bruce Hall, Annapolis, MD, Wiest historian

Brian Barr Wiest, *History and Genealogy of the Wiest Family*, 1975. It is interesting to the author that Brian Wiest visited his great grandmother, Sally Wiest Troutman, while researching his Wiest roots.

Robert Viguers compiled a Wiest family history, *Descendants of Martin Wust, 1617–2015*. The Wiest family group charts which follow are courtesy of Bob Viguers.

1844 – Eyster to Wiest

John and Elizabeth (Harter) Eyster sold their house and barn on 120 acres to Jacob Klinger Wiest (1826–1878). Jacob K. Wiest married Elizabeth Troutman (1825–1881). They were married by 1844, as attested by the birth of Harry T. Wiest, their first-born child. Jacob would have been 18 years old, and Elizabeth, his wife, would have been 19 years old. She was the daughter of Peter Troutman, who built the stone house down Spain. This may seem to be a bit young to be buying a farm with a new log house and barn; however, Jacob K. Wiest, the son of Samuel Wiest, came from a long line of established landowners in the Klingerstown area. The Wiest pioneers had purchased their lands from the grandsons of William Penn.

The following paragraphs describe some Wiest family genealogy.

Jacob Wiest III, born in Oley 1775, died at Klingerstown in 1811, married Barbara Fick on July 31, 1793. Barbara Fick was born in 1774 and died in 1853. Jacob and Barbara resided on farmlands, which is recalled today as the Eston Klinger-Ivan Klinger farm. This property extends from the St. Michael's church location to the Klingerstown Hotel. The farmhouse is presently being remodeled in 2019 by the family of Mike and Peg Wiest.

Samuel Wiest, son of Jacob Wiest III, born 1795 and died 1867, resided 1/2 mile west of Klingerstown on the farm where Roland Romberger Jr. lives today. Samuel was a farmer, butcher, logger, and cattleman married Eva Klinger. Eva was the daughter of Peter and Catherine Steinbruch Klinger.

John K. Wiest, son of Samuel, above, was born in 1821 and married Beisel. He resided where Terry and Marla Williard reside today.

Jacob K. Wiest, son of Samuel, above, was born in 1826 (see below).

Jestina, daughter of Samuel, above, was born in 1828 and married William Schertel.

Jacob Klinger Wiest, son of Samuel, above, was born at the Roland Romberger farm. He married Elizabeth, daughter of Peter and Elizabeth (Batteiger) Troutman. Jacob was a farmer and a livestock man who lived on a farm of 120 acres, subsequently the property of George L. Troutman, who purchased it in 1881. Jacob K. Wiest and Elizabeth Troutman Wiest had 11 children. Elizabeth was killed by lightning while walking in the kitchen.

Jacob Beisel Wiest, son of John K. Wiest and Lucetta Beisel Wiest, lived at the Terry and Marla Williard residence. This Jacob founded the Wiest Logging Company near Portland, Oregon.

William Beisel Wiest, son of John K. Wiest and Lucetta Beisel Wiest, became president of the Wiest Logging Company in Portland, Oregon, and operated a wheat ranch near Lethbridge, Alberta, Canada.

Log house built in 1836 and barn built in 1840 by John S. Eyster (1786-1853)

Sold to: Jacob K. Wiest was born in 1826, and Elizabeth was born in 1825.

The first child born to Jacob and Elizabeth Wiest was born in 1844. John S. Eyster would have been 58 years old at the time of the marriage of Jacob and Elizabeth Wiest.

The estimated date of the photo is 1865.

People in the photo in front of the house from right to left: Mother, Elizabeth (36), Catherine (14), Jacob (6).

People in the photo in front of the yard fence from left to right: Father, Jacob K. Wiest (35); Edward (11); Frank (14); Samuel (8); Mother, Elizabeth (1825–1881); Father, Jacob (1826-1878);

Catherine (1851 who married Edward Witmer); Jacob (1859–1887); Edward (1854–1927); Frank (1851-1925); Samuel (1857–1928).

Note: The small white building adjacent to the log house marks a site that is possibly the earliest dwelling place of the Harter family. Old crockery was found at this location.

After the death of Elizabeth Troutman in 1881, by a lightning strike in the log house, the Jacob K. Wiest descendants sold the farm to John Troutman of the Hebe-Pillow area. Jacob K. Wiest (1826–1878) would have been deceased several years before Elizabeth was struck dead.

1881 – Wiest to Troutman

Jacob Klinger Wiest (Wust) was born June 23, 1826, near Klingerstown, and was christened on September 16, 1826, at Klingers Church. The sponsors were Peter Klinger and his wife, Catharina. On October 12, 1878, he died in Upper Mahanoy Township, Northumberland County, and was buried at Klingers Church. His tombstone is in row 15, number 377. Jacob married Elizabeth Trautman, daughter of Peter Trautman and Elizabeth Batteiger, about 1843. Elizabeth was born November 22, 1825, in Spain, Lykens Township, Dauphin County. She died July 29, 1881, in Jordan Township, Northumberland County. According to the Wiest book, page 205, she was killed by lightning while walking in the kitchen. Jacob and Elizabeth had the following children:

1. **Henry Trautman (Harry) Wiest** (November 24, 1844–April 1, 1917).
2. **John Trautman Wiest** (October 4, 1846–August 16, 1919).
3. **Amelia Trautman Wiest** was born about 1847.

4. **Frank Troutman Wiest** (September 24, 1851 – April 12, 1925).

5. **Catherine Trautman Wiest** was born about 1851. Catherine married Edward Witmer.

6. **Edward Trautman Wiest** (February 28, 1854 – 1927).

7. **Samuel Trautman Wiest** (1857–1928).

8. **Jacob Trautman Wiest** (January 28, 1859 – June 16, 1887).

9. **Monroe Trautman Wiest** was born in January 1864.

10. **Preston J. Wiest** (April 18, 1865 – March 16, 1916).

11. **William Trautman Oscar Wiest** (1867–1950).

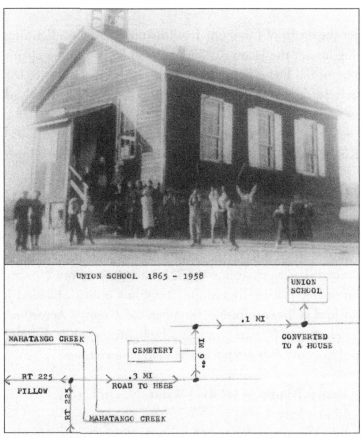

Union School, 1865-1958, located north of Union Cemetery. Pillow was previously known as Union Town. This school has been converted to a house.

CHAPTER 4

George L. Troutman Family

George L. Troutman and his son-in-law, John K. Romberger, rebuilt the barn and straw shed.

Ralph and Carrie Romberger compiled the *Troutman Family History*. Typed copies were distributed to family members. Their son, Dr. John A. Romberger, continued sharing the history and photographs. John's research contributed to this book. Note that George and Mary Troutman are the grandparents of author Steve E. Troutman. Earl and Marion Troutman are his parents.

Troutman History
by Ralph T. Romberger, February 14, 1970
George Lesher Troutman, born June 21, 1858, died October 7, 1934. On December 8, 1878, he married Mary Louise Wert, born December 17, 1856, died December 26, 1925. They are both buried in the Union Cemetery near Pillow. Children:

1. **Alice Amelia Troutman** married John K. Romberger. Child: Ralph Troutman Romberger.
2. **Victor William Troutman** married Sallie B. Wiest. Children: Leo Tobias, George Monroe, Mary Savilla, John David, Ray Clayton, Guy William, Allen Clair (died in childhood), and Harry Bryant Troutman.
3. **Dora Agnes Troutman** married William B. Wiest. Children: Mabel Louise, Helen Marie, Mark Woodrow, and Alice Elizabeth Wiest (died in infancy).
4. **Alvin Mark (?) Troutman** (died in infancy).

George L., son of John and Harriet (Lesher) Troutman, was born and brought up to farm life at the John Troutman homestead located in Jordan Township, Northumberland County. He attended the Union (Bohner's) School, No. 1, located about one and one-third miles west-northwest of the homestead, and about one mile northeast of Pillow, a small town in upper Dauphin County.

George was married on December 8, 1878, to Mary L. Wert, daughter of William and Catharine (Riegle) Wert. The Werts were also farm people and lived on a farm of about 143 acres located in Upper Paxton Township, Dauphin County, about three-fourths of a mile northeast of Killinger. As Mary's father, William Wert, had died in August before George's and Mary's marriage, Catharine Wert (Mary's mother) needed a farmer. George and Mary started housekeeping in the tenant house on the Wert farm, which they worked until sometime during 1880.

Following this, they moved to a small home located (on the south side of the road) about fifty-two normal steps southeast of the David's

House and barn of George L. Troutman and Mary L. Wert, remodeled in 1898.

Lutheran and United Church of Christ at Hebe. The above home was owned and occupied by David Adam Reed. While living there, George was employed by his half brother Simon, a farmer and drover, who lived about one-eighth of a mile north-northeast of the village.

In 1881, George and Mary moved to a farm of about 120 acres located on the road between Hebe and Klingerstown, also in Jordan Township. George obtained this farm from his father, John Troutman. It was formerly the homestead of John Eister, who built the house in 1836, and the barn in 1840. This farm was owned by the Victor W. Troutman Estate and is occupied by George M. Troutman, grandson of George L. and Mary L. Troutman. George and Mary were engaged in general farming and were numbered among the prosperous farmers of their community. They tried to keep the farm buildings in good condition and remodeled both house and barn during 1898. Also, in 1907 an addition called "the straw shed" was built to the barn on the south side. This greatly increased the barn's storage capacity, which was sorely needed.

George was of medium stature and build, neither stout nor slim. He was a good provider in every way and was interested in gardening

Troutman Family, *left to right*: Victor, George L., Mary L. with Dora in lap, and Alice.

and the growing of tree fruits, such as apples, cherries, peaches, pears, and plums. George was a very good hand at picking blackberries, also at the gathering of huckleberries on the nearby mountain ridges. During October, he liked to gather generous amounts of the common American chestnuts, which are almost extinct. George enjoyed long walks occasionally, such as to Sunday School picnics at Red Cross, and at Himmel's Church located near Rebuck in the Schwaben Creek Valley, also other places. George and Mary have been identified among the congregation

Troutman Family, *left to right*: Victor, George L., Alice, Mary L., and Dora.

of the Troutman's United Evangelical Church, of which his father was the founder. In political sentiment, George was a Republican.

From the spring of 1903 until sometime during 1920, George and Mary had their son-in-law, John K. Romberger, and his wife, Alice A., work the farm for shares. Following this, George and Mary had no steady tenant farmer. Mary died at the Troutman homestead on December 26, 1925, where she lived for almost forty-five years. In November 1926, George disposed of household goods at a public sale, and on December

1, 1926, he sold the farm to Samuel B. and Sarah Joanna Wiest, who lived on the adjoining farm to the north.

George then resided with the Wiests on the old Troutman homestead for some time. Later one of the Wiests' sons, namely Howard (Eugene), and George lived together at several different places over several years, including Lykens, Donaldson, and Klingerstown. George also lived with his grandson Ralph T. and wife, Carrie E. Romberger (about one mile northwest of Klingerstown) for some time, but mostly with his son Victor W. and wife, Sallie B. Troutman, near Klingerstown. There, he died from the effects of cancer on Sunday, October 7, 1934, at the age of 76 years, three months, and 16 days.

Recap of Troutman History
by Ralph T. Romberger (March 13, 1965)

1881	George L. Troutman and Mary L. Wert moved to Jordan Township farm of 120 acres.
1898	George L. Troutman rebuilt the house and barn.
1903–1920	John K. Romberger and Alice Troutman, George's daughter, are tenant farmers for George and Mary.
1907	A large addition to the barn is added on the south side. The new addition is named the straw shed. This addition was completed when the Rombergers were the tenant farmers.
1926	George L. Troutman sold his farm to Samuel B. Wiest.
1935	Victor Troutman, son of George L, purchased the farm where he was born and raised. His son, George M. Troutman, and family moved on the farm soon after that.

Recent tenants include Antonio and Jane Michetti, Joseph Troutman, Jr., Greg and Tatianna Berdi, Mervin and Verna Esch, Mark Yerger and Jeanelle. The Esch's lived at the property for approximately one year.

They kept livestock in the barn and held a church service in the top of the barn. During the church service, 40 horses were stabled in the barn.

The "meeting house" was built as a school house in 1840. When the public schools were built in 1865, the building was converted to Troutman's United Evangelical Church. Church services were held there until about 1920. After that it was used as a storage shed until about 1970 when it was torn down for road improvement.

George L. Troutman was born here on the John Troutman farm, presently Lenker Farms, between Hebe and Pillow.

The "Little Red House" (Tenant House) on the George L. Troutman Farm in 1920 (looking southeast).

This posed picture was made at 12.45 P.M. on June 4, 1920, by Ralph T. Romberger. The people sitting on the porch were (left to right): Eva Shutt (a hired housemaid), Carrie E. Bahner Romberger, and John Klinger Romberger.

The road in the foreground is the Klingerstown to Pillow Road, which was not paved until 1936. Though traffic was rather light in 1920, road dust was an unpleasant consequence of this location in summer and fall.

My father, Ralph T. Romberger, lived in this small house with his parents from April 1903 until 1910, when he moved across the road to the "Big House" to live with his grandparents, George L. and Mary Wert Troutman. His parents continued to live in this "Little Red House" until 1920 when his mother, Alice A. Troutman Romberger, died on February 15 during the flu epidemic. My parents also lived here for a short time after they were first married in 1918, and then again briefly in 1920. (John A. Romberger)

The "Little Red House" (Tenant House) on the George L. Troutman Farm in 1920 (looking southwest).

This posed picture was made at about 1:00 P.M. on May 27, 1920, by Ralph T. Romberger, my father. The figure on the porch is my mother, Carrie E. Bahner Romberger. Though not clearly visible, it seems that she was standing by a pump, as though she had been drawing a pail of water. The porch, the well, and then the house were abandoned shortly after widening and paving of the road in 1936 made the location untenable. (John A. Romberger January 2006)

Came E. Bahner Rombeiger Cooking in 1920. (My mother in the kitchen of the 'Little Red House' on the George L. Troutman farm).

This picture was taken in the kitchen of the tenant house (the "Little Red House") on the George L. Troutman farm in late February or early March of 1920 (after the death of Alice Troutman Romberger). Such stoves were typical in farm kitchens of that time. They were usually fired with wood in the summer and with hard coal in the winter. These stoves had ovens suitable for baking bread, pies, and cakes (but had no automatic temperature controls or timers). The boxy right end of this stove contained a water tank with a capacity of about ten gallons. This provided a supply of moderately hot water for handwashing and dishwashing. However, water for cooking, coffee, or tea, was typically heated on the stove in a large cast-iron teakettle, such as the one seen here. Note the barn lanterns (fueled by kerosene, which was then known as coal oil) on the shelf behind the stove. Before the days of rural electricity, these were an absolute necessity. This photo is somewhat unusual for its time in that it shows a person seemingly at work rather than just posing (John A. Romberger).

Alice Amelia Troutman was born on August 15, 1880, and died on February 15, 1920. On January 13, 1900, she married John Klinger Romberger (June 17, 1876 – January 16, 1954). They are both buried in the Maple Grove Cemetery at Elizabethville. Their child, Ralph Trout-man Romberger, married Carrie Elsie Bahner.

Alice was the oldest child and first daughter of George L. and Mary L. (Wert) Troutman. They lived in Hebe, situated in the Mahantango Valley, Jordan Township, Northumberland County. While living in Hebe, George and Mary occupied a small home located (on the south side of the road) about fifty-two normal steps southeast of the David's Lutheran and United Church of Christ. At that time, (Alice's father) George was employed by his half brother Simon Troutman, a farmer and drover who lived about one-eighth of a mile north-northeast of the village.

This formal portrait of Alice Amelia Troutman was prob-ably made on her 18th birthday (August 15, 1898), but we have no documentation of the actual date.

In 1881, George and Mary moved to a farm consisting of about 120 acres, also in Jordan Township, Northumberland County. This farm is located about one and one-half miles (by road) west-northwest of Klingerstown (situated in Schuylkill County). George obtained the above farm from his father, John Troutman.

Alice attended the local schools, mostly the Noble (Rothermel's) School, No. 4, located about one-half mile east of the Troutman homestead and about one mile northwest of Klingerstown. She also attended the Grove (Hebe) School, No. 3, for some time. This school was located about two-thirds of a mile west-southwest of the homestead, on the Klingerstown-Hebe road and along Trout Run (called *Farrella Ruhn* by the Pennsylvania Dutch). The above were both one room, little red schoolhouses, typical of that time. Alice, however, secured a fair education in those schools. By her parents, she was trained to do both house and farm work efficiently and later became a model farm woman.

Alice was married on January 13, 1900, to John K. Romberger (June 17, 1876 – January 16, 1954). John was the youngest son of William and Susanna (Klinger) Romberger, who lived in Gratz, Dauphin County. By occupation, William was a cabinetmaker and undertaker's helper. John's parents both died from tuberculosis before he was fourteen months old. His mother's parents were Daniel and Anna(Schoffstall) Klinger, who lived on a farm a short distance southeast of the Klinger's church, located near Erdman, in Lykens Township, Dauphin County.

William Romberger's parents were Christian and Susannah (Matter) Romberger. They lived on a farm where some of the acreage, in the area where the buildings stood, was owned by C. J. Umholtz, D.D.S., of Elizabethville. The farm was located about two and one-half miles northwest of that town and only a short distance north of (what used to be) Herman's school. Christian Romberger's parents were (Heinrich or Henry) and Elizabeth (Hoffman) Romberger. It is believed they lived in the Lykens Valley, as most of their children were baptized at Hoffman's church, which was located between Gratz and Berrysburg.

In the spring of 1900, Alice and John started housekeeping in Washington Township, Dauphin County, on the farm, then owned by Michael R. Keiper. The farm buildings and the farm in part were owned and occupied by James J. Lebo. This farm is located about one half mile northeast of Elizabethville on the Loyalton road, also known as State Route 209. They farmed there as tenants for almost three years, specializing in dairy farming. They delivered milk to Elizabethville daily by one-horse wagon. When Alice began delivering milk, the gray horse named Bill knew many stops better than Alice did. When hitched to the hayfork, this same horse needed no driver or anyone to lead him; he obeyed the spoken words. While farming, John, with a grain cradle, mowed seven acres of oats in one day.

On April 3, 1903, Alice and John moved into the tenant house on her parents' farm and began working the home place for shares. This farm was owned by the Victor W. Troutman Estate and was occupied by George M. Troutman, grandson of George L. and Mary L. (Wert) Troutman. While working the Troutman homestead, they did general farming, not specializing in any particular crop. However, they raised more pigs than the average farmer did at that time.

While living on the Troutman homestead, John, who had learned the butcher trade in his youth, in the winter months, did many farm and home butchering of both cattle and hogs, for relatives and neighbors in the Klingerstown area. Occasionally, Alice helped to butcher for others too. They usually did at least two butcherings, at their home, during the winter season. Bony cuts of meat were lightly salted and used during the winter season. Some pork and beef sausage, also pork loin was canned in one-quart glass jars. Liverwurst (or pudding) was made; it was delicious but rather greasy. Scrapple (or *ponhaus*) was also made at butchering time; the supply was usually gone too soon. Home-cured meats were mostly used during the warm weather season. Many pork shoulders and hams, also pieces of pork bacon, were cured and smoked, as well as homemade summer sausages. Dried beef, cut from the rump of beef, was also cured and smoked; if sliced thin, it was very delicious. Several four- and five-gallon crocks were also filled with salted down pork and beef sausage for frying. Of course, they had to be soaked in water (for about twenty-four hours) before frying to get rid of most of the salt.

Without enough acreage with Alice's parents' farm of about 120 acres, John and Alice decided to buy a farm of their own for additional acreage. It happened that neighbors living about two-thirds of a mile southeast of the Troutman homestead had their farm for sale. This farm owned by Rufus M. Savidge and wife Laura E. Savidge, containing about 156 acres (plus 10 acres timberland in Lykens Township, Dauphin County), was purchased on April 17, 1912, for $3,000. The buildings on this farm are located about three-fourths of a mile (by road) to the south of the Klinger-stown-Hebe road, in Jordan Township, Northumberland County. The above farm was owned by Ira I. and Florence M. (Rothermel) Hoffman.

When the above farm was purchased, most of the buildings were in a run-down condition and needed attention. The house, barn, implement shed, and corncrib all needed new roofs and other repairs. A new chicken house was built, and later a new granary. After several years, the farm buildings were renovated and painted. The farm home then compared with the average farmstead in the area.

The farm roads were also rebuilt, and the clogged drainage ditches in the low-lying land were opened. Thus, by better drainage, better crops were produced. Alice and John were both good managers and hard work-ers. Consequently, the farm was greatly improved within a short time. Alice usually had a maid, and John, one or two hired boys as helpers. During haymaking time and wheat harvest, as well as during cornhusk-ing season, they usually hired extra help if it was available.

John and Alice, for many years, had seven workhorses and a few colts. John was a good horseman, and it seemed he liked to train colts and young mules. Young growing cattle were usually kept on the Rom-berger farm. Sometimes steers were also fattened there. Usually, about nine or ten milk cows were kept on the Troutman farm. After milk-ing, the warm milk was run through a cream separator (hand-powered), which skimmed the cream from the milk. The skim milk, while still warm, usually was fed to calves and pigs. The cream was ripened, and butter was then produced by churning the ripened cream. All milk was then worked out of the butter by the process of kneading. Worked butter was then molded into prints of about one pound each and wrapped in a special parchment paper. Hucksters then bought the butter from the farmers, also eggs and other farm produce, which they sold in the nearby coal region towns.

Alice and John, some years, also raised ducks or geese, and sometimes a few turkeys on the Troutman farm, as it was more convenient to tend them there than on the Romberger farm. Alice always did most of this work. Of course, her father, George L. Troutman, usually took care of the chickens.

Alice and John often raised quite a plot of onions in the low-land on the Romberger farm. Early potatoes, cabbage, tomatoes, sweet corn, cauliflower, watermelons, cantaloupes, and cucumbers were also raised. Sweet potatoes were usually raised on the Troutman farm because better attention could be given to them.

Alice was of medium height and build, neither slim nor stout. She was a fine mother and a very competent housewife in every respect. Alice was kind-hearted, had a friendly personality, and was well-liked wherever she was known. She was an upright, just woman and had an excellent Christian character. Her favorite hymn was "What a Friend We Have in Jesus," which she sang quite frequently.

Alice was an exceptionally good homemade bread baker; at her house, bread was seldom bought from the baker. The fried (egg) bread, with onions, and the jelly-rolls she made were second to none. Alice was an excellent cook, and it did not take her long to make a good meal. She was also good at sewing and made a lot of her own clothing.

Alice never cared much for recreation by travel and had never been farther from home than to the Gettysburg National Military Park. However, she attended some local Sunday School picnics and camp meetings. John and Alice sometimes attended the Gratz Fair, and on one occasion, they attended the Milton Fair, in northern Northumberland County. On May 8, 1915, they attended the Barnum and Bailey Circus at Sunbury.

Alice and John were both members of the Troutman's United Evangelical Church and attended church services there frequently. This church was located about two miles east-northeast of Pillow. In political matters, John was a Republican, and Alice never had the opportunity to vote.

Alice and John had one son, namely: Ralph T. Romberger, who married Carrie E. Bahner, daughter of Adam F. and Sarah E. (Hain) Bahner. To this union were born two children: Marie L. Romberger, who married first, Clarence W. Brosius (this union was dissolved by divorce), and who married secondly, Clarence (Charlie) A. Enders; and John A. Romberger, who married Margery J. Davis.

Alice contracted influenza and pneumonia, and after a short illness, died on Sunday, February 15, 1920, at the Troutman homestead, during the severe influenza epidemic prevalent at that time. On the following Friday, February 20, she was buried in the Maple Grove Cemetery at Elizabethville. John was also very sick with influenza at that time and could not attend his wife's funeral. John's brother, Harry K. Romberger, took care of him on the funeral day. John's recovery was slow and was drawn out over many weeks.

At the end of the funeral, the snow was quite deep, and the roads were severely drifted and were impassable at many places. Such places were avoided by following the sleigh tracks through the fields. The funeral party traveled on three two-horse sleighs via Hebe, Pillow, and Berrysburg to Elizabethville. The foremost sleigh (driver, Allen S. Rothermel) carried Alice's pastor, Rev. Grant H. Seidel, and the pallbearers. They were: David W. Strohecker, I. Monroe Rothermel, Andrew J. Schwalm, and Allen S. Rothermel. The second sleigh, drawn by two black horses (drivers, the funeral director George F. Buffington, and his helper), carried the casket. The third sleigh (driver, William A. Romberger, who was John's brother) carried, besides the driver, the following: Harry C. Romberger, John's nephew; Florence M. Rothermel, who later became the wife of Ira I. Hoffman; Adam F. and Sarah E. Bahner; and Ralph T. and Carrie E. Romberger.

After a short graveside service, the funeral party retired for dinner (noon meal) to the Washington Hotel, located on the northeast corner of Main and Market Streets in Elizabethville. The horses were fed in the spacious shed in which the hotel conducted a hostler service. There was a large horse watering trough, with running water, on North Market Street, on the hotel building's west side. There was adequate hotel service for the occasion, and the trip back to the Troutman homestead was made without incident. The weather was frigid on the funeral day; however, it did not snow.

A suitable monument and headstone of pink-colored granite were erected on the cemetery lot at Elizabethville. During the spring of 1920, a two-horse load of topsoil from Alice's onion plot was hauled on the lot to help get grass started. Following Alice's death, John continued farming for George L. and Mary L. (Wert) Troutman until the fall of 1920.

As the influenza epidemic was quite bad when Alice died, only a brief funeral service was held at her parents' home. Therefore, on Sunday forenoon, June 6, 1920, a memorial service was held for Alice in the United Evangelical Church at Pillow. Her former pastor, Rev. James K. Hoffman, preached the memorial sermon, which was very well attended.

On August 28, 1920, John married, secondly, Blanche E. (Hoffman) Klinger. Their children were: Jean E. Romberger, who married Richard Malnick; and Betty J. Romberger, who married Earl F. Kohr. On Tuesday, September 7, 1920, John disposed of livestock and farm equipment at a public sale held on the Troutman farm. Sometime during the following November, John moved to Tower City. He was then engaged in the buying and marketing of farm produce (an occupation known as huckstering at that time).

Farm out buildings include a grain storage building, pig stable, corn house, and chicken houses.

After living in Tower City and huckstering for several years, John decided to purchase a garage, including equipment, in Loyalton. John and Blanche operated the garage for some time. However, due to hard times, they were in business there for only a few years. Following this, they moved to another place in Loyalton, where they lived for some years. After living there for some years, they moved back to Tower City. While living there in January 1954, John had a bad fall on the porch and down the steps at the home where they were then living. He was then taken to the Pottsville Hospital, Pottsville, Pennsylvania, where he died on January 16, 1954, at 77 years, six months, and 29 days. At the time of his death, John was a member of the Methodist Church in Tower City. He was buried in the Maple Grove Cemetery at Elizabethville.

Dora Agnes Troutman (July 21, 1888 – October 21, 1927) married, June 4, 1906, William Baum Wiest (February 19, 1883 – April 19, 1962). They are both buried in the Union Cemetery near Pillow. Children:
1. **Mabel Louise Wiest** was born on May 11, 1908. She married, June 11, 1927, Irvin Dey Williard, born on July 17, 1906. No children.

Johannes Harter Homestead. William Wiest Jr. seated, Helen and Mark Wiest with their doggies.

2. **Helen Marie Wiest** was born on October 24, 1914. She married November 3, 1946, William Aloysius Gallagher, born on January 28, 1901. The Gallagher union was dissolved by divorce on August 26, 1953. Child: Patricia Eileen Gallagher, born on January 7, 1948.

3. **Mark Woodrow Wiest**, born on June 21, 1917. He married June 8, 1940, Lillian Irene Nornhold, born on November 8, 1918. Children: Alice Anne Wiest, born on December 28, 1944; Mary Ellen Wiest, born on August 24, 1948.

4. **Alice Elizabeth Wiest** (March 14, 1922–April 9, 1923).

The George Lesher Troutman Family in the Fall of 1906.

The probable occasion of this family photo was the marriage of George and Mary Troutman's youngest child, Dora Agnes, to William Baum Wiest, Jr., in June 1906. This newly married couple was planning to move to Lebanon, Pennsylvania, in the fall. This picture was probably taken in September or October, as the leaves are still on the trees, but the geraniums have already been taken indoors (visible in the window).

The people left to right are: Back row, John Klinger Romberger (June 17, 1876–January 16, 1954), Alice Amelia Troutman Romberger (August 15, 1880–February 15, 1920), Victor William Troutman (June 2, 1882–December 25, 1947), Dora Agnes Troutman Wiest (July 21, 1888–October 21, 1927), William Baum Wiest, Jr. (February 19, 1883–April 19, 1962). Front row, Mary Louise Wert Troutman (December 17, 1856–December 26, 1925), George Lesher Troutman (June 21, 1858–October 7, 1934), Sallie Baum Wiest Troutman (July 31, 1882–August 16, 1972). Standing in from George is his grandson, Ralph Troutman Romberger (December 29, 1900–June 20, 1974). Sitting on Sallie's lap is her son Leo Tobias Troutman (October 7, 1905–April 13, 1980).

The site of this family portrait was the lawn near the southeast corner of the George Troutman farmhouse, which is still relatively unchanged today. This picture has been in my family, packed away in a box, for as long as I can remember. I had it framed and now have it hanging in my study (John A. Romberger).

Dora was born at the Troutman homestead, located in Jordan Township, Northumberland County, about one and one-half miles (by road) west-northwest of Klingerstown. She attended the Noble (Rothermel's) School, No. 4, located about one-half mile east of the homestead and about one mile northwest of Klingerstown. This was a one-room little red schoolhouse, typical of that era. Dora quit school before she was fourteen years of age; however, she attained a fair education by continued effort in home study. Dora was brought up to farm life and became a very efficient housekeeper in every way.

Dora was married on June 4, 1906, to William Baum Wiest, Jr., born February 19, 1883, and died April 19, 1962. William B. Wiest, Jr. was a son of William Baum Wiest, Sr. and Elizabeth Baum Wiest, his wife. The parents of William B. Baum Wiest, Jr. started housekeeping on a farm in Powell's Valley, Dauphin County, and lived there for some time. Their next move was to a farm located about two miles (by road) west-northwest of Klingerstown on the Hebe road, in the Mahantango Valley, Jordan Township, Northumberland County. There William B. Wiest, Jr.

was born. This farm is now (1967) owned and occupied by George R. Wolfgang. After farming there for some years, William B. Wiest, Sr. and the family moved onto a small farm located in Lykens Township, Dauphin County, near Erdman, where they lived for about one year. Following this, they moved to the Klingerstown Hotel and conducted the hotel business in that town for some time. While they lived there, Elizabeth died. Later, William B. Wiest, Sr. moved onto a farm located on the right bank of the Mahantango Creek, about one-fourth of a mile north-northwest of the square in Klingerstown. This farm is partly in Jordan Township, Northumberland County, and partly in Upper Mahantango Township, Schuylkill County. It was owned and occupied by Clarence (Tol) Ray Williard. Later, William B. Wiest, Sr. went to Alberta, Canada, where some family members had lived at one time or another. Following this, years later, it is said William B. Wiest, Sr. was murdered at a hotel in Shelby, Montana.

William Baum Wiest, Sr. and Tobias Baum Wiest were brothers, whereas their wives, Elizabeth Baum Wiest and Mary Ann Baum Wiest, were sisters. William B. Wiest, Jr. and Sallie B. (Wiest) Troutman were first cousins on both the family's paternal and maternal sides. William B. Wiest, Sr. was born and raised on a farm (owned by Samuel B. Wiest during the 1920s) located about one and three-fourths miles (by road) northwest of Klingerstown, in Jordan Township, Northumberland County. Samuel and Hettie (Baum) Wiest were the parents of William B. Wiest, Sr. Samuel was reared in Klingerstown, where William R. Romberger lived. Samuel, the father of William B. Wiest, Sr., was accidentally killed while felling a tree in the wood lot on the Weist homestead, located about one and three-fourths miles (by road) northwest of Klingerstown. This Samuel Wiest's parents were John and Catherine (Merkel) Wiest.

In the fall of 1906, Dora and William started housekeeping on North Fourth Street in Lebanon because William had secured employment with the Bethlehem Steel Company there. After a while, due to the excessive heat in the steel plant, William decided to start farming.

And so it was that, in the spring of 1907, William and Dora started farming for shares for Mrs. Mary (Straub) Baum on her farm located about one-third mile west of Klingerstown. After farming for some time, William and Dora decided to go homesteading in the province of Alberta, Canada. In the late winter of 1907-08, they disposed of their livestock, farm equipment, and household goods at public sale.

Following the sale, in the early spring of that same year, William started (by train) for Lethbridge, Alberta, Canada. Dora stayed with her parents, while William traveled ahead to take up a quarter section of land (160 acres) and built a small house. Arriving in Lethbridge, William then took up a quarter section some forty miles to the north of that place, in the vicinity where the town of Travers is located. Some Wiest family members had emigrated to Alberta before William, and no doubt, they gave him some assistance in his settlement. William purchased and hauled enough lumber from Lethbridge to his quarter section some forty miles distant, to build a small house. Although he had plowed a fire break around his lumber and building site, a prairie fire on a stormy day crossed the fire break and burned nearly all his lumber for the house. Undaunted, William bought some more lumber to build a small house.

While William was trying his best to start farming and build a house, Dora, at the home of her parents back in Pennsylvania, on May 11, 1908, gave birth to a daughter named Mabel Louise Wiest, who in later years became the wife of Irvin D. Williard. When the daughter was about four months of age, in early September 1908, Dora started (by train) from Herndon for Lethbridge, Alberta, Canada, to join her husband. The trip was a hard one with the small child; however, both mother and daughter safely got to Lethbridge. When Dora and her daughter arrived in Lethbridge, Worth Wiest (brother of William B. Wiest, Jr.) was in town (with a team of horses) to get some lumber. Nevertheless, he took Dora and her daughter along on the lumber wagon to William's homestead.

In the area where William and Dora settled, the main crops raised were spring wheat, oats, and a little hay. Field corn was not raised as the growing season was too short. While William and Dora lived there, it was very dry in some years, and the yields of grain were poor; therefore, they finally decided to return to Pennsylvania.

In the late fall of 1912, the William B. Wiest family returned to Pennsylvania. Mabel was about four years and seven months old at that time. For the next several months, the Wiests stayed with Dora's parents. During the winter of 1912/13, William and Dora purchased from William A. Zerbe the farm consisting of about 48 acres where William Jr. was born in Jordan Township, Northumberland County. This farm is on the Klingerstown-Hebe road about two miles west-northwest of Klingerstown and adjoined Dora's parents' farm in the west. At an earlier date, William's father had owned the above farm. It was owned and occupied by George R. Wolfgang. In about 1913, William and Dora also purchased from William A. Zerbe, a timberland tract containing about 10 acres near Erdman.

In about 1916, William and Dora bought from Paul A. Updegrave a farm consisting of about 77 acres. This arm, then locally known as the "Schadel Farm," is located slightly less than a mile (airline) northeast of Hebe in Jordan Township, Northumberland County. While living on this farm, in October 1927, Dora died. The farm was later sold to Albert T. Strohecker.

Around 1920, William and Dora purchased a farm consisting of about 140 acres from Frank and Charles Balsam (brothers). This farm is located about three-fourths of a mile southeast of Hebe in Jordan Township, Northumberland County. In about 1930, this farm was sold to Jacob W. Strohecker and was since owned by Earl G., Bruce A., and Bryant A. Troutman, all brothers. They named the farm "Green Acres." Bruce A. Troutman and his family occupied it. At one time, William also owned the large double house in Hebe locally known as the "Big House."

Dora was fairly tall and medium in build. She was a good mother and provided well for her family at all times. Dora was a hardworking woman and a conservative, efficient housekeeper in every way. She was outspoken when she had something to say; however, that might be the better way after all. Dora was rather stern but good-natured at heart. Dora and William were both well known in their home community and were numbered among its substantial citizens.

William was a Democrat in politics; however, it is not known that Dora ever voted. William was a member of the David's Reformed Church, since called the United Church of Christ, at Hebe. Dora died at the Schadel Farm on October 21, 1927. She had been affected by double pneumonia.

Pneumonia is seemed rather prevalent in the family. Dora and William and their daughter Alice E. died in infancy and are buried in the Union Cemetery near Pillow, in Jordan Township, in lower Northumberland County, about three-fourths of a mile northeast of the town.

Quite sometime after Dora had died, William entered into a common-law marriage agreement with Polly Sophia (Wolfgang) Land. They lived together at several different places, including a farm between Herndon and Red Cross in Jordan Township, Northumberland County. A son, Stanley James Wiest, was born to them on February 27, 1931. Among his other farms, William had purchased (about 1930) a small farm consisting of about 9 acres from Charles A. Bohner. This small farm is located about two-thirds of a mile (airline) north-northeast of Hebe. There in his old age, William resided with his son Stanley and wife for several years. William was admitted to the Northumberland County Hospital near Shamokin, Pennsylvania, shortly (about twenty-four hours) before his death, which occurred there. William is buried in the Union Cemetery near Pillow.

Dora and William were parents of four children, three daughters, and one son, in order as follows: Mable Louise, Helen Marie, Mark Woodrow, and Alice Elizabeth (died in infancy) Wiest.

William Wiest Jr. and Dora owned several farms. This farm adjoined her parents' farm on the west.

Troutman History

by Michael Troutman, son of Daniel Troutman

Ada Klinger Troutman, the wife of John D. Troutman, resided with her husband on the Victor and Sally Troutman farm of Troutman Brothers. She and John had married when she was 16 years old. Ada moved to live with her husband's people. She often recalled Sally telling the story of so many family descendants who had passed away at the residence of Victor and Sally Troutman. This was the old Baum log house that became the Wiest home of the next generations and is now recalled as the Victor Troutman home residence. Sally Troutman took care of old George L. when he was a widower. His wife and two daughters had predeceased him. It was the natural state of events at that time for George to live with his son Victor. Victor's wife, Sally, cooked, washed, and cared for her father-in-law, most remarkable as told by Sally. She cared for old George for 11 years, 11 months, and 11 days. This timely account is the courtesy of Michael Troutman, son of Daniel and Nancy Troutman. He lived next door to Sally.

Rothermel's School, as it appeared in 1923. It was also known as Noble School. It was one of 7 schools built in Jordan Township, between 1864 and 1865. This school house was located near the old Billie Rothermel homestead, presently the residence of Joe and Ruby Michetti.

CHAPTER 5

Wert Family History

Ralph Troutman Romberger (December 29, 1900–June 20, 1974). Date of this photograph–November 28, 1961.

Compiled in 1968 by Ralph T. Romberger and Carrie E. Romberger. Photographs, captions, and additional Wert history, by Dr. John A. Romberger.

THE WERT FAMILY

The name is variously spelled Wert and Wirt, sometimes by members of an immediate family. The early forebears, it has been found, spelled the name Wirth. These early settlers were especially friendly with the Indians, and in some cases, lived among them.

Someone has said, "History is an open window through which we can look back into the past." Therefore, we shall now attempt, by word pictures, to let you look back into the Wert family history.

No person is aware of the difficulties and perplexities experienced in collecting and arranging the history and lineage of a large family, except those who have tried it. Some errors have inevitably crept into the history, but the effort has been made to make it as nearly correct as possible.

In preparing this work, we believe that family history, no matter how accurate and complete in its birth, marriage, and death dates, will become monotonous without the addition of historical, biographical, and anecdotal material. Thanks are due, and much credit must be given to many persons for their valuable help and the information they gave, used in this work.

John Adam Wirth (as the name was then spelled), the first of this line to come to America from Germany, and the pioneer ancestor, was born in 1727 in Germany. According to *Rupp's Collection of Thirty Thousand Names of Immigrants in Pennsylvania* (1876), he landed at Philadelphia on September 28, 1753, on the ship *Two Brothers* (Thomas Arnot, Captain. Sailed from Rotterdam, Netherlands, last from Portsmouth, England). He was the progenitor of the family in Dauphin County, having come to this county in 1768 from Lancaster County. John Adam Wirth settled near Killinger, among the Indians, and his farm was the site of an Indian village. He became very friendly with the Indians, and they showed him every courtesy. In the early settlement, a wounded Indian was brought to his home, whom he and his family nursed back to health, and the gratitude of the Indians was shown in their every action after that. Wirth was one of the five original settlers of the Lykens Valley. He prospered well and finally became the owner of about 1200 acres, divided among his sons. He also gave a farm to the Reformed congregation, now (1963) called the United Church of Christ, and one farm to the Lutheran Church, of which he was a member.

His wife, Eva Elizabeth Wirth, was born in Germany in 1730. She bore him the following children: George, Christian, Jacob, Adam, and Joseph, also one daughter who married Daniel Stever, a soldier in the Revolutionary War (another account states this, "These pioneers had nine sons." However, the daughter is not mentioned). The sons mentioned above settled in different parts of the country. The family became scattered over New Jersey, the Carolinas, Ohio, and through the West, besides having many Pennsylvania representatives. John Adam Wirth died in 1806, and his wife Eva Elizabeth Wirth died in 1800. They are both buried in the "old" Lutheran Cemetery at Killinger.

John Wert II, the father of Henry, lived in the Lykens Valley about two miles above Millersburg. Henry Wert (or Wirt) was a pioneer farmer of the Mahantango Valley, Northumberland County, having settled in that section when the Indians still roamed the forests. The red men were neighborly with "Henner" Wert, to whom they bade farewell when they left the region. He and his wife Elizabeth are buried side by side in the Zion's (Stone Valley) Lutheran and United Church of Christ Cemetery near Hickory Corners, in Lower Mahanoy Township, Northumberland County.

The Wert family ancestors, who lived in the lower Lykens Valley area, were very friendly with the Indians in pioneer times, and the Indians respected them highly. The Werts, along with the Indians, used the same spring and bake oven occasionally, and sometimes the Indians camped along the same stream in which the Werts watered their livestock.

On one occasion, a group of Indians came to one of the Werts, who had settled in what is now the Killinger area. The Indians complained bitterly about how they had been cheated in a fur and hide deal with a particular settler. The man in question lived near what was later known as Woodside Station, located about two and three-fourths miles east-southeast of Millersburg and on the north side of Berry's Mountain.

They told Wert they were going over to scalp the man. Because it was late in the afternoon, Wert asked the Indians to stay with him for the night. They accepted the invitation, and Wert decided on a course of action. Wert did not sanction dishonesty and cheating; nevertheless, he wanted to prevent bloodshed if possible. During the early evening and night, he gave the Indians all the hard cider they could drink. Succeeding in getting them drunk, be hurriedly sent his hireling on horseback to warn the settler to flee. And flee, he did. When the Indians came to do their scalping, the settler was not to be found.

THE WILLIAM WERT FAMILY

William Wert was born in the Lykens Valley in upper Dauphin County on January 11, 1821. He died on August 25, 1878, at 57 years, seven months, and 14 days. He was the son of Daniel Wert (December 7, 1796 – October 20, 1858) and his wife Susannah (Shoop) Wert (March 21, 1797 – March 12, 1873). Daniel Wert and Susannah Shoop (parents of William Wert) were married on April 26, 1818. One account stated, "They had eight sons and five daughters." However, William Wert had at least two brothers, who were named, Isaac and Daniel.

William was married on January 1, 1846, to Catharine (Ketty) Riegle, a daughter of Benjamin and Catharine (Deibler) Riegle (see THE BENJAMIN RIEGLE FAMILY). Catharine (Riegle) Wert was born on August 9, 1828, and died July 11, 1907, at 78 years, 11 months, and two days. The Werts are both buried in the cemetery adjoining the Riegle's Evangelical United Brethren church, in Mifflin Township, Dauphin County, Pennsylvania. However, William and Catharine, both were members of Jacob's Church of the United Brethren in Christ at Killinger. This church is now (1964) called Jacob's Evangelical United Brethren Church.

The Werts started housekeeping and farming on a farm consisting of about 143 acres, located in Upper Paxton Township, Dauphin County, about three-fourths of a mile northeast of Killinger, a short distance to the south of the Millersburg-Berrysburg road now (1964) State Route 25. When William and Catharine got possession of the farm, a short distance in a westerly direction of the farmhouse, across a small stream,

William Wert, Father of Mary Louise Wert, in about
1872. The original of this photographic portrait was
made in about 1872 by J. S. Aunspach in his Pillow
studio. The print that I copied is a small 2 by 3-inch
oval on light-weight printing-out paper pasted onto
a 2.5 by 4-inch mount. An Aunspach serial number
4550 appears on the back. This print was #31 in
a collection of Wert-Troutman photographs that I
inherited from my father.

there was a spring the Indians had crudely walled with stone. Later the
water from this spring was piped to the spring (or tenant) house on the
Wert farm. Near this spring, an Indian corn pounding mortar (made of
stone) was found, and many arrowheads were picked up in the area.

The Werts did general farming, including raising sheep for wool and
growing flax for fiber. In her younger years, Catharine did home spin-
ning of flax, which was common in those days. Flax is an annual plant,

ripening in ten to twelve weeks, growing (on good soil) to a height of about forty inches. The plants were pulled by hand, carefully dried, and the seed removed with a flax hackle (or heckle). The straw was then either spread out upon the ground and exposed to dew and rain or submerged in water for a few weeks to undergo a process of fermentation known as "retting." The straw was then dried, and the fiber separated from the bark and the woody portion of the stem by "breaking," a process that broke the brittle portion of the stems, making possible its separation from the tough, flexible fibers.

During Civil War days, William was drafted for military service in the Union Army, at which point he hired Baltzer Ritzman as a substitute to serve in his stead. The Werts paid him the sum of $300, plus the best horse in the barn, and signed an agreement to the effect that should he become disabled in the military service; the Werts would take care of him as long as he lived.

The threshing of grain was mostly done in the late fall, often when it was quite cold. The Werts daughter, Mary L. (later Mrs. George L. Troutman), occasionally had her feet frostbitten while helping to thresh grain on the barn floor. They used a one-horse treadmill to run their crude threshing machine, which consisted of a spiked cylinder and a shaker arrangement to separate the grain and chaff from the straw. The grain and chaff were later run over a hand-powered fanning mill to separate the grain from the chaff. That part of the work was often done in the evening, candle burning lanterns being used to furnish the meager light. The amount of wheat threshed and cleaned in one day usually did not exceed fifteen bushels.

William was a Republican in political sentiment, and on one occasion, had been a candidate for county commissioner of Dauphin County. He was an exceptionally honest and hard-working man, and, as well as being a farmer, he was also a farm implement dealer. During land clearing operations, William accidentally cut himself in one leg with an ax. The cut healed slowly and contributed greatly to his untimely death.

Following William's death, Catharine had tenants work the farm. For some time, George L. Troutman and his wife, Mary L. (Wert) Troutman, cultivated the farm. Later, Catharine's son, William A. Wert, and his wife, Emma I. (Hennaman) Wert, worked the farm. There were two houses on the farm, now (1964), still standing, the tenants had occupied the smaller one. Sometime while Catharine was having the farming done by her son and his family, due to brush burning in a nearby field, a straw stack accidentally caught fire, setting fire to the barn, which burned to the ground. However, the barn was soon replaced by a new one.

Catharine was numbered among her community's substantial citizens and was widely known in the Lykens Valley area. She had an excellent managerial ability; however, she was rather stern, although good-natured at heart. Catharine was of a tall build, and during her later years, she was quite stout. She was a hard-working woman and an efficient housekeeper in every way.

William and Catharine (Riegle) Wert were the parents of seven children, two sons, and five daughters, in order as follows:

1. **Amanda Jane Wert** (February 9, 1847–August 21, 1913) married on June 9, 1868, James Peter Hoy (September 27, 1843–March 18, 1914).
2. **Aaron Benjamin Wert** (September 29, 1848–March 1, 1862).
3. **Emma Catharine Wert** (October 24, 1850–September 2, 1930) married on October 1, 1871, John Henry Matter (April 13, 1851–June 12, 1916).
4. **Sarah Elizabeth Wert** (March 31, 1853–March 31, 1915) married on January 30, 1873, Jeremiah Lebo (May 1, 1851–June 2, 1933).
5. **Mary Louise Wert** (December 17, 1856–December 26, 1925) married on December 8, 1878, George Lesher Troutman (June 21, 1858–October 7, 1934).
6. **William Albert Wert** (May 28, 1863–January 25, 1932) married on October 11, 1884, Emma Ida Hennaman (November 6, 1864–May 4, 1930).

7. Alice Amelia Wert (July 6, 1865–May 2, 1944) married on April 19, 1884, Charles Franklin Shoop (December 14, 1861–June 2, 1921).

Mary Louise Wert as a Young Lady in about 1874. The original of this portrait was made by C. H. Snively in his Millersburg studio, probably in about 1914. It is about 2.5 by 3.5 inches. Someone long ago trimmed the picture with a scissors to fit an album space. The back of the mounting card (some of which was cut away) bears the Snively name and the serial number 10453. It also bears a penciled number 36, probably added by my father after acquiring a collection of Mary Wert's pictures from Sallie Troutman (Victor Troutman's widow) in about 1965.

Mary Louise Wert was a daughter of William and Catharine Riegle Wert. She had four sisters and two brothers. She and her siblings were raised to farm life on the William Wert homestead just east of Killinger in the Lykens Valley of upper Dauphin County. This is the site of the present Harrisburg North Golf Resort.

As a young girl, Mary Louise did housework and barn and fieldwork along with her father and some of her sisters. Her older brother, Aaron Benjamin, died when he was only 13. Her father died prematurely at 57 (in 1878) after suffering years of partial disability, after an accidental ax wound in a leg. Mary Louise's younger brother William A. Wert eventually grew up and took over the farm's operation from their mother Catharine in about 1881.

Mary Louise often told her grandson, my father, how they threshed and cleaned their grain in the late fall and winter using a crude threshing machine powered by a one-horse treadmill. They then cleaned the grain by running it through a hand-cranked "fan mill." They had to work a whole day in the cold, even sometimes suffering frostbite, to prepare 15 bushels of wheat for the market.

We have not yet learned how Mary Louise Wert met George L. Troutman, but we can speculate that it was probably at a church meeting, as they belonged to different congregations of similar Evangelical churches only about 15 miles apart.

Mary Louise Wert married George Lesher Troutman. They had three children, of whom Alice Amelia (August 15, 1880 – February 15, 1920), my paternal grandmother, was one. She died on the old George Troutman homestead, where she had lived for more than 40 years, on December 26, 1925, the day after I was born (John A. Romberger).

John Lesher Troutman (May 26, 1860–January 27, 1906) and George Lesher Troutman (June 21, 1858–October 7, 1934) were two of the 15 children of John Troutman [the elder] (June 10, 1817–March 22, 1901). Two of these children were born by John's first wife, Sarah Lesher (October 19, 1817–April 4, 1841), who died when only 23. The other 13 were born by his second wife, Harriet Lesher (December 16,

John Lesher Troutman (left) and George Lesher Troutman (right) as boys in about 1870. The original of this photograph is a small 2.25 by 3.5 inches pasted onto a slightly larger mount. The back of the mount bears the Aunspach logo but no serial number. This photograph dates, I think, from about 1870. A penciled "61" was probably added by my father. There are also glue marks indicating that the picture was once mounted in an album (having black pages). Sometime, long ago, the print was damaged by creasing, as is still evident.

1824–April 27, 1888). Both Lesher women were daughters of Samuel Lesher (March 12, 1782–March 12, 1844). They were half-sisters because Sarah's mother was Samuel's first wife, and Harriet's mother (Mary Magdalene Smith/Schmidt) was his second wife.

John L. Troutman and George L. Troutman, along with their numerous siblings, grew up on the John Troutman [the elder] homestead farm in Jordan Township of Northumberland County (but only about two miles east of Pillow, which is in Dauphin County). This Troutman homestead farm was just over the hill to the south of another Troutman farm occupied by my maternal grandparents, Adam and Sarah Hain Bahner, and their children (a sharecropping farm family). Because of various intermarriages between Bahners, Troutmans, and Leshers, both of my parents are descendants of the same early Troutman and Lesher settlers.

George L. Troutman grew up to marry Mary Louise Wert on December 8, 1878. Further details of this couple's marriage and their offspring appear above.

John L. Troutman, though of a seemingly jovial disposition, and well-liked by his neighbors, the Bahners, never married. Sometime in the late 1890s, John L. and an unmarried sister, Magdalene (b. March 25, 1843), were given the old homestead farm by their aging father. However, this odd couple, younger brother and a spinster sister seventeen years his senior, did not make a good farming team, and they hired a tenant to work the farm. Magdalena, though, was a good housekeeper, cook, baker, and seamstress, and she undoubtedly took care of her younger brother, almost like a mother would have. Sadly, like her mother, Magdalena became obese, her health failed, and on July 13, 1905, she died at the age of 62. John L. Troutman did not adjust well to the loss of his sister. Then in the winter of 1905/06, John's disposition turned gloomy and, before anyone took this seriously, he committed suicide by hanging himself in the barn. This happened on Saturday, January 27, 1906. My mother remembered that shocking event. That barn is still in good condition and is still in use.

CHAPTER 6

Samuel M. Wiest Family

1. Samuel M. Wiest, 2. John B. Wiest 3. Samuel B. Wiest, 4. Eugene Erdman.

From Wiest to Troutman to Wiest

In 1926, George L. Troutman sold his farm to Samuel B. Wiest, also known as Butcher Sam Wiest. The following documentation is based on genealogical work provided by other Wiest historians, including Robert Viguers and Brian Wiest. Both men have provided extensive Wiest history.

We will begin with Samuel Merkel Wiest (1819–1866), the son of John Wiest and Katharina (Merkel) Wiest of Klingerstown, a wealthy businessman and property owner of many farms in the Klingerstown

Samuel M. Wiest, father. Sons are Tobias B. Wiest, John B. Wiest, and William B. Wiest.

Samuel B. Wiest, "Buther Sam," son of William B. Wiest. Earlier Samuel M. Wiest.

area. Samuel M. Wiest was the grandson of Jacob Wiest III, the Mahantongo Valley pioneer who married Barbara Fick.

Samuel M. Wiest lived on what is recently known as the Eugene Erdman farm. He married Esther Baum, daughter of John Baum Jr. and Elizabeth Drumheller. John Baum Jr. was born and raised on the farm now Troutman Brothers.

Samuel M. Wiest had many sons. John Baum Wiest (1863–1935) succeeded to his father's farms in Jordan Township after his father was killed at a relatively young age by a fallen tree while timber harvesting on the farm. A sawmill presently is located and operated in this vicinity by the sons of Eugene Erdman.

John was married to Hannah W. Strohecker, the daughter of William Strohecker and Sarah Sally Wiest. John Baum Wiest had the Wiest family wanderlust and moved to Lethbridge, Canada, to farm wheat about 1910. He sold his father's Jordan Township farms to Samuel B. Wiest, the son of his brother, William Baum Wiest (1852–1918), who was murdered in Montana in 1918. John and Sarah Wiest are buried at Union Cemetery, Jordan Township.

Samuel Baum Wiest (1878–1957), son of William Baum Wiest and Elizabeth Baum (daughter of David Baum, who lived on the farm which

George L. Troutman, farm house, John K. Romberger, tenant house, and a farm building called the "gschroder house" where animal feed was processed by grinding grain and corn.

is now Troutman Brothers), was given the name Butcher Sam Wiest to distinguish him from other Sam Wiests. It is of interest to note that William Baum Wiest Jr. was married to Dora, the younger daughter of George L. Troutman. At Troutman Brother's butcher shop, John D. Troutman often spoke of Butcher Sam Wiest, who sold meat door to door with a horse and wagon when he was a boy growing up on the Victor Troutman-Sally Wiest farm. This is now the home of Troutman Brothers.

The Wiest brothers Tobias and William married Baum sisters. Tobias B. Wiest, son of Samuel M. Wiest, married Mary Baum, also a daughter of David Baum.

William and Elizabeth's son, John Carlos Wiest, was raised by Mary Baum on the Troutman Brother's farm after her sister, Elizabeth, died. There are photos of John C. Wiest in military service as a soldier in World War I with the 1st US Infantry.

Samuel Merkel Wiest (1819–1866)

Samuel Merkel Wiest was born on November 19, 1819, in Klingerstown. He died on February 20, 1866, in Klingerstown and was buried at Klingers Church. He was a farmer and butcher and resided two miles northwest of Klingerstown. His descendants are sometimes called 'Hetta' Wiests. According to the 1850 Census, he was a laborer worth $2000 with a wife and three children. Samuel married Esther Jette Baum, daughter of Johannes Baum Jr and Elizabeth Drumheller, about 1842. Esther was born on September 17, 1820. She died on May 26, 1910. Samuel and Esther had the following children:

1. Infant Wiest was born on October 12, 1843, in Jordan Township, Northumberland County. She died on October 15, 1843, and was buried at Klingers Church.
2. **Tobias Baum Wiest** was born on August 10, 1844, and died on February 13, 1912. Tobias married Mary Baum.
3. **Jonathan Wiest** was born on July 6, 1846. He died on October 19, 1861, and was buried at Klingers Church.
4. **May Jene Wiest** was born on February 14, 1851.

5. **William Baum Wiest** was born on August 4, 1852. William married Elizabeth Baum. He was murdered in 1918 in Shelby, Montana.
6. **Aaron Wiest** was born about 1854.
7. **Richard Wiest** was born July 9, 1855, in Hebe. He died March 13, 1877, and was buried at Klingers Church.
8. **Samuel Markel Wiest Jr** was born on September 27, 1857, and died on December 12, 1877.
9. **Libarius Baum Wiest** was born on April 7, 1860, and died on November 13, 1888.
10. **John Baum Wiest** was born in July 1863 and died in 1935. He succeeded to his father's farms.
11. **Amelia Wiest** was born in 1866 and died in 1940.

John Baum Wiest (1863–1935)

This record identifies John, the son of Samuel M. Wiest. John took over the management of his father's farms after Samuel was killed in the woods. However, as stated below, John had other interests in going to Canada. He transferred his inherited farms to his nephew, Samuel B. (Butcher) Wiest. John Baum Wiest later returned to the area. The 1880 Census lists him living with his mother, Esther, and his stepson Wesley Troutman. He was buried in Union Cemetery, Jordan Township, Northumberland County. John married Sarah Hannah Strohecker, daughter of William Strohecker and Sarah Sallie Wiest, about 1882. Sarah was born on May 26, 1861, in Hebe. She died on March 18, 1940. John and Sarah had the following children:

1. **Jennie Mae Wiest**
2. **Samuel Elmer Wiest**
3. **William Allen Wiest**
4. **Beulah May Wiest**
5. **Clarence Ray Wiest**
6. **Laura Alverta Wiest**
7. **Emma Wiest**
8. **Lola Wiest**

Tobias Baum Wiest (1844–1912) married Mary Ann Baum (1848–1931)

Tobias was born and raised on the farm lately recalled as the Eugene Erdman farm, 1½ miles northwest of Klingerstown. Tobias operated farms in Klingerstown, where Troutman Brothers is now located. The following family group chart courtesy of Robert (Bob) Viguers of Harrisburg:

1. Theobald Baum (1693–1762), Alsace Township, Berks County.
2. Johan Peter Baum (1718–1794).
3. John Baum Sr. (1754–circa 1800 in the Mahantongo Valley).
4. Heinrich Baum (1786–1866). He was buried at Klinger's Church. His twin, Helena, drowned in the Schuylkill River. Henry married first Catherine Sterner (1784–1820), second Salome Gundrum (1795–1852).

5. David Baum (1816–1893) married Susanna Welker (1819–1893).
6. Mary Ann Baum (1848–1931) married Tobias Baum Wiest (1844–1912), buried at Klinger's Church.

Tobias Baum Wiest was born on August 10, 1844, in Hebe. He died on February 13, 1912, in Klingerstown and was buried at Klingers Church. He married Mary Ann Baum, daughter of David Baum and Susanna Welker, about 1868. Mary was born in 1848. She

Mary Ann Baum Wiest poses near her home on Troutman Brother's farm. John D. Troutman recalled this story. When he was a baby, his grandmother, Mary Ann, would chew crackers in her mouth and then place them in baby John's mouth, to learn to eat solid food.

Mary Ann Baum Wiest, the mother of Sally Troutman, d. December 20, 1931, aged 83y. 6m. 10d. known locally as "Die Alt Tobsin."

died on December 20, 1931, in Klingerstown. Tobias and Mary had the following children:

1. **Emma Clara Wiest** was born on April 21, 1869, in Klingerstown. She died on October 24, 1914, in Klingerstown and was buried at Klingers Church. Emma married Jacob Dimmler. Jacob was born about 1869 in Frackville.

2. **Samuel Baum Wiest** was born on February 15, 1871, in Klingerstown. He died May 3, 1871, in Klingerstown, and was buried at Klingers Church.

3. **John Baum Wiest** was born on January 12, 1873, in Klingerstown. John married Sevilla Wiest, daughter of William Beisel Wiest and Myrith Paul. Sevilla was born on November 29, 1878.

4. **Katharine Baum Wiest** was born on January 5, 1876, in Klingerstown, and christened March 12, 1876, at Klingers Church. She died December 7, 1891, in Klingerstown and was buried at Klingers Church.

5. **Sally Baum Wiest** was born on July 31, 1882, and died on August 16, 1972.

6. **Monroe Baum Wiest** was born on March 5, 1885, in Klingerstown. He died in May 1970 in Schuylkill Haven and was buried in Union Cemetery, Jordan Township, Northumberland County. He was a woods foreman and lived in Eagle Creek, Oregon.

7. **David Baum Wiest** was born on January 22, 1889, in Klingerstown, and was christened April 24, 1889, at Klingers Church. He died December 29, 1891, in Klingerstown and was buried at Klingers Church.

Sally B. Wiest, photo by Elaine Moran. Framed charcoal portrait under glass.

John Baum Wiest 1873–1945

John Baum Wiest, born January 12, 1873, a son of Tobias Baum Wiest, married Sevilla Wiest Wiest (1878–1945), the daughter of William Wiest. This William Wiest descended from John Wiest and Samuel Wiest of Portland, Oregon. John was vice president of the Wiest Logging Company of Portland and resided in Sellwood, a Portland suburb. John and Sevilla are buried in Greenwood Hills Cemetery, Portland, Multnomah County, Oregon.

Tobias Wiest family photo by Annspach, a photographer from Pillow. Monroe, father Tobias Wiest, Sally, mother Mary Ann (Baum) Wiest, John C. Wiest (nephew of Mary Ann). John's mother, Elizabeth, died young in 1892. His father, William Baum Wiest, died in Shelby, Montana, in 1918 when he was murdered in a hotel. John C. Wiest (Jolie) was a veteran of WWI.

Circular family photograph hanging in the parlor at the Sally (Wiest) Troutman house. Sally Wiest, Monroe Wiest, Emma (Wiest) Dimmler, John Wiest, Savilla (Wiest) Wiest, wife of John, who resided in Sellwood, near Portland, Oregon. Emma resided in Fountain Springs, near Ashland.

Samuel M. Wiest, Mary Ann Baum album

John S. Geise (1864–1944) married Emma S. Geise (1867–1940). From a Fitting Studio portrait in about 1888. Restoration by John A. Romberger, Dec. 2007. Earl Troutman recalled the funeral day. The Hebe Church bell tolled for the years of his age. Earl heard the bells from his home.

William Baum Wiest (1852–1918)

William Baum Wiest was a farmer and hotel operator in Klingerstown for many years. After his wife died, he moved to Alberta, Canada, where he engaged in the meat business in Travers, Canada. His wife, Elizabeth, was a sister to his brother Tobias's wife, Mary Ann. As mentioned previously, William B. Wiest was murdered in Shelby, Montana, and is interned in Alberta, Canada. His wife, Elizabeth (Baum) Wiest, born January 4, 1852, was the daughter of David BAUM and Susanna Welker. William and Elizabeth married in 1876. She died on December 14, 1892, and is interred at Klingers Church Cemetery. William and Elizabeth had the following children:

1. **Mary Jane Wiest** was born on June 22, 1875.
2. **Richard Elder Baum** was born on February 26, 1877, and died in 1960.
3. **Samuel Baum "Butcher" Wiest** was born in 1878 and died in 1957. He is buried at Union Cemetery.
4. **Worth Baum Wiest** was born about 1880 and died about 1936.
5. **Clara Wiest** was born about 1881.
6. **William Baum Wiest Jr** was born on February 19, 1883, and died on April 19, 1962. He married Dora Agnes Troutman, the daughter of George L. Troutman. He is buried at Union Cemetery.
7. **Ella Wiest** was born about 1885.
8. **Elizabeth Wiest** was born about 1887. Elizabeth married George Orian Wiest, son of John Beisel Wiest and Sarah N. Herring, about 1905. George was born about 1875.
9. **Ira Baum Wiest** was born on September 29, 1889. He died on March 6, 1893, in Klingerstown and was buried at Klingers Church.
10. **John Carlos Wiest** was born on January 10, 1892, and raised by Aunt Mary Baum at the Troutman Brother's farm.

Samuel Baum "Butcher" Wiest (1878–1957)

"Butcher Sam" Wiest lived on the Eugene Erdman farm. He earned his nickname by his work. He operated a butcher shop on his farm, processing meat and meat products. Some of his butchering equipment is still in use today by the Eugene Erdman family. Butcher Sam's cooking kettles are still used to make scrapple. Butcher Sam was a nephew to John Baum Wiest, who earlier lived on this farmland. Butcher Sam Wiest purchased the George L. Troutman farm from George Lesher Troutman on December 1, 1926, when George retired. Butcher Sam later sold it back to the Troutmans, to Victor Troutman, the son of George L. Troutman. Butcher Sam's brother, William Wiest Jr., married Dora Troutman, the daughter of George and Mary (Wert) Troutman. William, the boy married Dora, the girl next door.

Another Samuel Baum Wiest was a hotel man in Valley View. He owned several farms in Klingerstown. Samuel Baum Wiest married Sarah Jennie Snyder, daughter of Peter Snyder, about 1898. Sarah was born in 1875 in Northumberland. She died in 1950. Samuel and Sarah had the following children:

1. **Homer Wiest** was born in 1900 and died in 1973.
2. **Howard Wiest** was also born in 1900. He also died in 1973 and was buried in Union Cemetery.
3. **Luther A. Wiest** was born on March 16, 1906, and died on March 5, 1975.

William Baum Wiest, Jr. (1883–1962)

The son of William Baum Wiest Sr., he married Dora, daughter of George and Mary Wert Troutman of Jordan Township. As a resident who became a rancher in Alberta, Canada, his interesting life is recorded in the book by Ralph Romberger. He returned to Klingerstown, where he became a large landowner of farms between Hebe and Klingerstown. William and Dora had children Mabel Louise, Helen Marie, and Mark Woodrow. Alice Elizabeth died in infancy. Mark's account of his father building a new house on the old Harter homestead is also included in this book. After Dora died in December 1927, William married Polly

Wedding Day. William B. Wiest Jr. married Dora Agnes Troutman. The photo is from Dora's childhood home. "Old" George Troutman Family – 1905. Front Row: Mary (Wert) Troutman, George L. Troutman (holding Ralph Romberger), Sallie (Wiest) Troutman (holding baby Leo Troutman). Back Row: John Romberger, Alice (Troutman) Romberger, Victor C. Troutman, Dora (Troutman) Wiest, Wm. (Billy) Wiest.

Sophia (Wolfgang) Land. A fourth child, Stanley James Wiest, was born on February 27, 1931. Local people recall Stanley as Toby Wiest.

William Baum Wiest married Dora Agnes Troutman, daughter of George Lesher Troutman and Mary Louise Wert, on June 4, 1906, in Berrysburg. Dora was born July 21, 1888, in Jordan Township. She died on October 21, 1927. William and Dora had the following children:

1. **Mabel Louise Wiest** was born on March 11, 1908, and was christened on June 7, 1908, in Berrysburg. Mabel married Irvin Dey Williard on June 11, 1927. Irvin was born on July 17, 1906.
2. **Helen Marie Wiest** was born on October 24, 1914.
3. **Mark Woodrow Wiest** was born on June 21, 1917.
4. **Alice Elizabeth Wiest** was born on March 14, 1922, and was christened on May 19, 1922, in Berrysburg. She died on April 19, 1923, and was buried in Union Cemetery.

Sources:

Ralph T. Romberger and Carrie Romberger compiled the *Troutman Family History.*

Dr. John A. Romberger continued sharing the history and photographs by his father,
Ralph T. Romberger

George and Mary Troutman, the grandparents of Steve E. Troutman

Earl and Marion Troutman, the parents of Steve E. Troutman

Bruce Hall, Wiest family historian

Bob Viguers, *Descendants of Martin Wust*

Brian Barr Wiest, *History and Genealogy of the Wiest Family*

GROVE SCHOOL ABOUT 1910

WILLIAM TROUTMAN WAS THE TEACHER. THE
SCHOOL WAS CLOSED ABOUT 1918 WHEN THE
HEBE SCHOOL WAS BUILD. THE BUILDING WAS
TORN DOWN AT THAT TIME FOR THE LUMBER.

HEBE BYPASS

CREEK

RT 225

Pillow

RT 225

MAHANTONGO

4.2 MI

ROAD TO KLINGERSTOWN

GROVE
SCHOOL

GROVE
This school was one of the first
to be abandoned and was located
between Noble and Hebe schools.
Old records list only seven schools.

Groves School about 1910. William Troutman was the teacher. The school was
closed about 1918 when the Hebe School was built. The building was torn down
at that time, for the lumber. Groves school stood at the intersection of Green Acres
Farm Lane and the Hebe- Klingerstown Road.

CHAPTER 7

Victor W. Troutman Family

Victor W. Troutman was born and raised on this farm.

Victor W. Troutman History
by Ralph and Carrie Romberger

Victor William Troutman, son of George L. and Mary L. (Wert) Troutman, was born June 2, 1882, and died December 25, 1947, at 65 years, six months, and 23 days. Victor was born at the Troutman homestead located in Jordan Township, Northumberland County, about one and one-half miles (by road) west-northwest of Klingerstown (which is situated in Schuylkill County). He attended the local schools, mostly the Noble (Rothermel's) School, No.4, located about one-half mile east of

The boyhood home of Victor W. Troutman.

the homestead and one mile northwest of Klingerstown. Victor also attended the Grove (Hebe) School, No.3, for some time. This school was located about two-thirds of a mile west-southwest of the homestead, on the Klingerstown-Hebe road and along Trout Run (called *Farrella Ruhn* in Pennsylvania Dutch). He attended summer school in Pillow for about six weeks. However, it is not known in which year. Victor also for some time (it is thought for one term) attended school at Elizabethville, in Dauphin County. While attending school there, he stayed with his aunt, Emma Catharine (Wert) Matter, and her husband John H. Matter, who lived at 37 West Main Street. Victor was reared to farm life and agricultural pursuits; however, he was also interested in constructing farm buildings and later became an efficient carpenter.

On September 22, 1904, Victor was married to Sallie Baum Wiest, who was born July 31, 1882. Sallie was the daughter of Tobias Baum Wiest and wife Mary Ann (Baum) Wiest. Tobias B. Wiest was born and raised on a farm (owned by Samuel B. Wiest during the 1920s) located about one and three-fourths miles (by road) northwest of Klingerstown, in Jordan Township, Northumberland County. Samuel and Hettie (Baum) Wiest were the parents of Tobias B. Wiest. Samuel was reared in Klingerstown, where William R. Romberger lived (1964). Tobias's father, Samuel, was accidentally killed while felling a tree in the woodlot on the Wiest homestead, located about one and three-fourths miles (by road) northwest of Klingerstown. Samuel Wiest's parents were John and Catharine (Merkel) Wiest.

David and Susanna (Welker) Baum were the parents of Mary Ann Baum. David Baum was born and raised on the farm, which was called the Spread Eagle Farm and was owned by Howard and Mary S. (Troutman) Williard. This farm is located about one-third mile west of Klingerstown. David Baum's wife, whose maiden name had been Susanna Welker, was a native of the Hoffman's Church area (located between Gratz and Berrysburg) in Dauphin County. Mary Ann Baum (wife of Tobias B. Wiest) was born at the Baum homestead owned by Howard and Mary S. (Troutman) Williard. However, in Mary Ann Baum's youth, her parents moved to the farm owned by Mrs. Sallie B. (Wiest) Troutman and adjoining the Baum homestead on the south. Henry Baum married Miss Steiner (or Stoner), both natives of Berks County, Pennsylvania. They were the parents of David Baum. Henry Baum was married twice. He secondly married his first wife's sister. This Henry Baum settled on the farm where Howard and Mary S. (Troutman) Williard lived. In the lowland, Henry first built a log house, a short distance southeast of the present dwelling, the second home built by Henry on this farm. Soon after the log house was built, both the Pine Creek (called Laurel Creek by the pioneers) and the Mahantango Creek (Kind Creek, so-called by the pioneers) flooded the low-lying area severely. Whereupon Henry decided to build a stone house (the Williards present residence) on higher ground.

Victor and Sallie started housekeeping in the tenant house, also known as the Gray House, on her parents' farm in the spring of 1905. Until sometime during 1908, Victor was engaged mostly in the trade of carpentry. During this time, he was mostly employed by Calvin C. Klinger of Klingerstown, a local contractor, who erected buildings as far away as the vicinity of Meiserville in Snyder County.

Following this, Victor and Sallie farmed for her parents, for shares, which included the Wiest homestead and about 50 acres of cleared land located about two miles (by road) northwest of Klingerstown. After the death of (Sallie's father) Tobias B. Weist, which occurred on February 13, 1912, Victor and Sallie worked the farms for her mother. Sometime during 1920, Victor purchased from W. Oscar Leitzel about 29 acres of land adjoining his mother-in-law's farm on the west. Mary Ann (Baum) Wiest died December 20, 1931, at her home in Upper Mahantango Township, Schuylkill County, Pennsylvania. Sallie then became the owner of her parents' farm of about 85 acres. The land located about two miles northwest of Klingerstown, in Jordan Township, Northumberland County, comprising about 50 acres of cleared land and about 70 acres of timberland had been disposed of an earlier date.

Victor was fairly tall. He was well built and was a hard-working man in every way. He was outspoken and did not hesitate to call a cat, a cat. However, Victor was good-natured at heart, had many friends, and was well known in his home community. On political questions, Victor was a Republican. However, he was not active in public matters.

Victor and his family did general farming; they also did considerable truck farming for market. In the late summer and fall months, farm produce was huckstered (or peddled) regularly in the nearby coal region towns, such as Donaldson, Tremont, Newtown, Branch Dale, and Llewellyn. Beginning about 1925, from about November to March, Victor started to sell from house-to-house, a good quality line of home-dressed meats and sausages, which proved to be highly successful. In August 1931, Victor and his sons started to butcher the year-round. The smoked sausage flavored with garlic and the ring bologna Victor put on the market were second to none. Early in 1935, Victor purchased the farm containing about 120 acres, where he was born and reared. (Victor W. Troutman purchased his boyhood home from Samuel B. Wiest, "Butcher Sam." Comment by Steve E. Troutman.) His son George M. Troutman and family moved on the farm soon after that. When beef cattle were purchased, they were usually stabled and fed on this farm and then killed as needed. The cattle were usually shipped by railroad or trucked from Virginia. At other times, the cattle were shipped from the Union Stock Yards in Chicago, Illinois. Early in 1935, Victor purchased the farm where he was born and raised.

Ray Troutman (1912–1989) and his biplane ca. 1938. The Air Circus at Troutman's Field often made the news!

Sometime during the early 1940s, Victor turned the butcher business over to his sons. The business has since been known as Troutman Brothers. Victor and Sallie were the parents of eight children, seven sons and one daughter as follows: Leo Tobias, George Monroe, Mary Savilla, John David, Ray Clayton, Guy William, Allen Clair (died in childhood), and Harry Bryant Troutman.

Victor was a member of the Reformed Congregation, called the United Church of Christ congregation, at Zion's (Klinger's) Lutheran and United Church of Christ, located about three-fourths of a mile (by road) southeast of Erdman, in Lykens Township, Dauphin County. Victor died suddenly on Christmas Day 1947 at the Troutman homestead located about one-half mile southwest of Klingerstown. Victor is buried in the cemetery adjoining the church of which he was a member.

The following tribute to Victor Troutman was published in the newspaper after a visit by Dr. Arthur Graeff (pen name 'N Ewich Yaeger) in 1939.

SCHOLLA AUS PENNSYLFAWNISH DEITCHLONDT
(Nuggets from the Pennsylvania Dutchland)
bei 'N Ewich Yaeger
(by The Eternal Hunter)

Troutman Barony (1939)

Victor Troutman's ancestors migrated from Oley and Tulpehocken to Klingerstown, Schuylkill County. Theobald Baum
of Oley was one of the early pioneers to cross the Kittatinny
Hills (Blue Mountains) and settle in the Penn domain known as
Spread Eagle Manor. The Troutmans came from Tulpehocken.
These two families settled on a huge tract of fertile land, which
borders on the west bank of the Mahantongo Creek. For four
generations, their descendants prospered on their island kingdom
of almost 300 acres.

Today Mr. Victor Troutman owns the entire island, and
prosperity still smiles upon the vast estate, which assumes the
characteristics of a self-sufficient barony.

Twenty-two buildings stand upon the Troutman farm. There
are stables, barns, garages (for 19 motor vehicles), a butcher shop,
a carpenter shop, a summer house, wash house, corns cribs, and
an old-time out-door baking oven.

Cakes, pies, and bread are still baked in the quaint old
oven, but by remarkable contrast, two airplanes are attached to
the private airport. Air flights are made to stockyards in Texas,
Kansas, and Chicago. Raymond Troutman, one of the five sons
of Victor Troutman, flies about the country, purchasing cattle for
the butchering business for the Troutman farm.

During some seasons, as many as 20 steers are slaughtered
each week on the Troutman farm, and seven delivery trucks sell
the meat to consumers within a 30-mile radius. Sixteen persons
are constantly employed in carrying on the many activities on
the farm. All these people prefer to speak in the dialect of their
Pennsylvania German forebears.

Mr. Victor has in his possession many ancient relics which his ancestors brought with them from Berks County. One especially interesting piece is a colonial rifle, with the name D. Bortz, carved into the steel barrel.

Some time ago, George Troutman, one of the five sons, decided to try out the old weapon. He used an ox horn to drop powder into the pan, inserted a bullet, wadded it with a grease patch, and rammed the ramrod into the chamber. Using the original flint on the hammer, he fastened the rifle to a tree, tied a string to the trigger, and pulled the string. The ancient gun barked in 1939 as it had barked at lurking Redskins a century and a half ago.

Victor Troutman is a feudal lord of his manor, and with one eye to his Berks heritage and the to the ultra-modern methods of farming, he preserves all that is best in culture and husbandry.

Victor Troutman and a two-team wagon. Victor Troutman on the wagon seat, Leo, standing on the wagon, Ralph Romberger, standing in front of the wagon wheel (Ralph is the father of Dr. John A. Romberger), Sally, holding George, the dog, Tobias Wiest, Mary Ann (Baum) Wiest, John C. Wiest, Jolie (raised by Mary Ann for her sister, Elizabeth) Baum Wiest.

Victor and Sally (Wiest Troutman, Leo, and George on a carriage. This photo was taken on the day they made a trip to Fountain Springs near Ashland to visit Sally's sister, Emma Dimmler.

(Author's Note: The preceding embellished account is essentially accurate, except for the second paragraph. John Baum's 300 acres had been divided in half before Victor Troutman arrived on the farm.)

Victor William Troutman, born June 2, 1882, died December 25, 1947. He married on September 22, 1904, Sallie Baum Wiest, born July 31, 1882. Children:

1. **Leo Tobias Troutman** married Katie Ann Fisher. Child: John Leo Troutman.
2. **George Monroe Troutman** married Mary Sarah Rabuck. Children: Earl George, Bruce Allen, Bryant Anson, and Clair Victor Troutman.
3. **Mary Savilla Troutman** married Howard Williard. Children: Pauline Agnes and Elwood Clayton Williard.

Children of Victor Troutman: Leo, George, Mary, John, Ray, Guy, and Harry.

Victor Troutman, 1882–1947, Sally (Baum) Wiest, 1882–1972 (photo by Earl G. Troutman).

4. **John David Troutman** married Ada Irene Klinger. Child: Guy (Johnny) Clifford Troutman.
5. **Ray Clayton Troutman** married first, Martha Irene Williard. (This union dissolved by divorce); married second, Mary Catherine Gelnett; married third, Kathleen (Kitty) Frances (Wilkinson) Aldinger. There were no children by either wife.
6. **Guy William Troutman** married Blanche E. Peifer. Children: Orpha Mae, Joseph Edward, Daniel Irvin, and Allen Guy Troutman.
7. **Allen Clair Troutman** died in childhood.
8. **Harry Bryant Troutman** married Amelia Ellen Wiest. Children: Ann Elizabeth, Karl Frederick, Emmy Lou (died in infancy), and Richard Ludwig Troutman.

Victor Troutman and his dog behind his butcher shop in Klingerstown.

CHAPTER 8

George M. Troutman Family

Recent Residents of the George and Mary Troutman Farm: Antonio and
Jane Michetti family; Joe Troutman Jr.; Tatianna and Greg Berdi; Mervin
and Verna Esch family; Mark Yerger and Jeanelle and families.

George (Pappy) Troutman in his new "Star" automobile.

Mary (Mammy) Troutman and a team of horses.

George, Mary, and Clair Troutman

The George Troutman family visiting his brother, John, at the Troutman Brothers farm in Klingerstown. George, Bruce, Earl, Bryant, and Mary.

George M. Troutman and the *Dengelschtock*. This was a pointed iron tool carried into the field. The tool was stuck in a log. It was pointed at one end. The top edge was then peened with a hammer to sharpen the cutting edge of the scythe.

The old Eyster log home as remodeled by the Troutmans.

Bryant, Earl, Clair, and Bruce Troutman with their dog Teddy.

Bruce Troutman with horses Jim and Dick and a two-row corn planter in the early 1940s.

Earl and Bruce Troutman

Bryant and Clair Troutman

Bruce and Earl Troutman on their ponies. They each have a six-shooter.

George L. Troutman and Mary (Wert) Troutman lived on this farm as an earlier generation.

Later, George M. Troutman and Mary (Rabuck) Troutman residence.

William and Catherine Shadle residence now owned by Tim Landis. Shadle's general store adjoining. The store was a two-story building with an addition (Clair Troutman photo collection).

William and Catherine Shadle store and outbuildings. Allen and Mae Rothermel residence (Clair Troutman photo collection).

CHAPTER 9

The Neighborhood

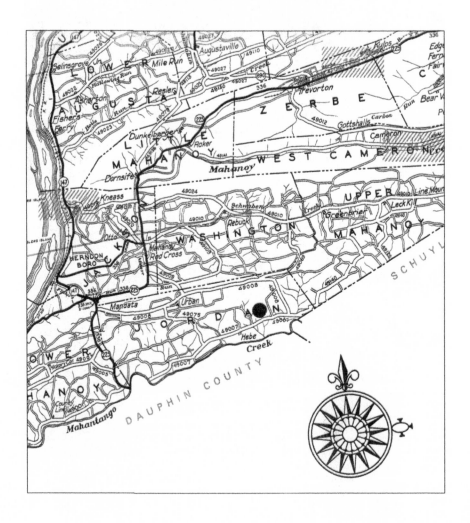

Cassy Patch

Phillip Lubold was a cobbler who resided on a small farm locally referred to as the Cassy Patch. This name originated with former property owner Catherine Shadle, a neighboring store owner. Florence (Rothermel) Hoffman and Ralph Romberger, old residents in the nearby area, recalled this Lubold residence. Ralph remembered it being in a deteriorated condition as a *Lumberei*, or rag mess. Earl Troutman purchased the Cassy Patch from the Shadles and built his family home nearby in 1963. Earl Troutman bulldozed the barn remains when he built his new house. The current residents are the Tim and Valerie Specht family. The Lubold family house location is marked by a hand-dug well and lilac bushes. A red and a black cherry tree stood nearby the barn.

Florence (Rothermal) Hoffman shared her early memories of living in this area where the pioneer Hartter family lived. She was born on the farm where she lived with her son, Robert Hoffman, just east of

This is the residence of Tim, Valerie, Emma, and Leah Specht. Their home borders the George and Mary Troutman farm. The view from the Specht home includes the Erdman and Landis farm.

A view from the former Earl Troutman residence, 2012, now the Specht Family residence since 2017.

the Hartter homesteads. Florence is the daughter of Manassas Rothermal. In 1914 Philip Lupold, a cobbler, lived south of the Earl Troutman residence on this tract of land. Philip was the last resident of this small homestead, but he was certainly not the first. Later, Mr. Lupold moved to the Hoofland area in the Fisher's Ridge Gap, approximately one mile north. There they built a house much like the one they left. The house is small and narrow, two stories high, with green shingles. It is close to the main road at the telephone exchange building. It is currently the residence of John Land.

Florence said she often walked by the Lupold house to visit her (paternal) Aunt Lull, who was married to Paul Kratzer. Paul and Lull Kratzer lived on the Hartter homestead farm in the new house, built by William Wiest Jr. Paul Kratzer was small in stature.

Florence said there was another house, now long gone, east of Bryant Troutman's residence, near the edge of the woods, several hundred feet south of the road leading to Florence's home. Only the location remains marked by a flat spot in Bobby's field where he found glass and crockery when tilling the soil. The water source remains as a spring in the hollow

Dr. John Romberger recalled the Phillip Lupold/Lubold house on the Cassy Patch was abandoned by 1927. John's parents, Ralph and Carrie Romberger, were neighbors. The Lubolds built this home in the gap of Fisher's Ridge after leaving Cassie Patch. This is currently the residence of John Land.

to the west. The names of any residents are forgotten, but the apple trees are remembered.

Peeler's Patch

This is a small tract of land bordering the George and Mary Troutman farm on the north. Earl Troutman purchased this property from Catherine Shadle. A hand-dug well was here as evidence of an earlier dwelling. Earl cleared the land of brush and closed the well. It was one of his first bulldozing jobs as a young man. The name George Hium is on an early survey in this book. The survey of Spread Eagle Manor shows the name Hium at the Peeler's Patch. Perhaps this name is Heim or Hime. There is a legend that the early Heim pioneers are buried in the garden of their home near Klingerstown. Mary Troutman recalled the story that there is a family burial plot on the Peeler's Patch. Mary said, *"Zwei kinner sind dat vergrabe."* (Two children are buried there.) Perhaps the Heim parents are buried here as well. Earl sold this tract to the Erdman family.

George Heim Jr.'s residence in 1790–1800.

In his *Geographical and Biographical Annals of Northumberland County, Pennsylvania,* Floyd described a tract of land that George Heim Sr. purchased from the Indians, which was "a large strip of land which extended from the Himmels Church in the direction of Klingerstown."

A proposed George Heim Jr. family dwelling is located along Erdman Farm Lane. This Jordan Township road is not the western boundary of Spread Eagle Manor, but the road approximates the boundary of the west side of Spread Eagle Manor. This road leads to the Peeler's Patch.

The Peeler's Patch is a possible George Heim Jr. homestead where the Heim family burial plot was in the garden. The Peeler's Patch in Jordan Township is a portion of Dr. Cadwallader Evans' tract of 262 acres. It was located between the Himmels Church in Washington Township, Northumberland County, and Klingerstown.

Kocher's Loch (Kocher's Hole)

This is a locale west of the Eugene Erdman family farm, close to Fisher's Ridge. A legendary Kocher family lived here, although no one can identify any dwelling remains.

Balsam's Loch

Balsam's farm was lately known as Green Acres farm, owned by Earl, Bruce, and Bryant Troutman. Robert and Lori Scott live on a portion of this farm today. It has also been referred to as Possum Hollow. Tim and Valerie Specht have a campsite on a portion of this farm adjoining the Mahantongo Creek at the confluence of Tumbling Run. More information on the Balsam family is included in this book on page 11.

Shadle's Store

William and Catherine (Strohecker) Shadle resided near the intersection of Erdman Farm Road and Klingerstown Road. Tim Landis is the current owner. The Shadles operated a general store next to their home in a separate building closer to the intersection. The store building had storefront windows and a porch with steps. The store sold necessities, food and dry goods, and tobacco and candy. Sometime in the 1960s, the Shadles had a sale. John and Agatha Troutman purchased the place and raised a large family there. The Shadles moved to Malta, where they operated a store near St. Luke's Church.

John Geist

When the author was a boy at the home of Earl and Marion Troutman, our closest neighbors were Allen and Mae Rothermel. They lived at the bottom of our driveway on Klingerstown Road. They lived in a small cottage built by John Geist. John had built the residence as his own. John built another house nearby at the intersection of Hooflander Road and Klingerstown Road. At the completion of this house, it was sold to the author's grandparents, Stanley and Verna Romberger. It seems John Geist did the same as John Eyster. They built houses for sale. Earl Troutman remembered hearing the church bells peal in Hebe for the funeral of John Geist. Other residents of John Geist's house included Ralph and Carrie Romberger, Harry and Amelia Troutman, and Tim Landis. Tim Landis removed the cottage and built a new house in the same location.

John Geist built this house, lately the residence of Tim and Jackie Landis. Other residents included Ralph and Carrie Romberger, Harry and Amelia Troutman, and Allen and Mae Rothermel.

Allen Rothermel's outbuildings and new Landis home under construction.

Toby Wiest

Stanley (Toby) Wiest lived in a log house on the Hebe Bypass. His house was constructed of reused logs. These logs were previously used in the Harter dwelling constructed on the Bruce Troutman farm, currently the farm of Lori and Robert Scott. Stanley Wiest's father, William, was first married to Victor Troutman's sister, Dora. He had three children with Dora. They built the house where Triston Scott lives today. William Wiest married second, Sophia Land, and Stanley was born.

First Clark Place

John and Samuel Clark lived in a log house residence on the George Wolfgang farm. This is currently the residence of the Burtons. This farm neighbors the George and Mary Troutman farm on the west. Clarks intermarried with the Baumans, who lived neighbors to the north.

Bauman Log House

Jacob and Maria Bauman/Bowman were some of the earliest in the vicinity known as Hebe. The old log house is still standing but abandoned. The property adjoins the George Wolfgang farm. The Strohecker family owns the pioneer dwelling. Access to this farm is from the Hebe Bypass, with a lane beginning near the Toby Wiest place. The log house was last

Jacob Bauman log house on the Hebe Bypass. Valerie, Emma, and Leah Specht are posing.

used as a migrant camp in the 1960s by the Stroheckers when they grew tomatoes for the cannery. The old Bauman log house has two hand-dug wells and is built on a higher elevation, not near any springs. Kocher's Loch borders this area to the east. Mathias Harter is named as a neighboring resident on an early survey. Jacob and Maria Bauman are buried in David's Cemetery as some of the earliest burials. The old log church building is now replaced with a stone church.

CHAPTER 10

Mary Ann Baum Photo Album and Photo Gallery

The home of Monroe B. Weist. Monroe was the son of Mary Ann Baum and Tobias Wiest. Troutman Brothers Farm, Klingerstown, Pennsylvania.

Mary Ann Baum married Tobias Wiest. Mary Ann is the daughter of David Baum and Susanna Welker.

Mary Ann's photo album remains in fair condition. It is in possession of the Troutman Brothers. Mary Ann and Tobias resided west

Mary Ann Baum was born here on the Spread Eagle Farm, the current residence of Elwood Williard Jr. (see page 115).

of Klingerstown on the old Baum homestead, presently Troutman Brother's Inc.

Several pictures from this album are included in this book elsewhere. They are pictures of Samuel M. Wiest, George Geise, and Mary Ann Baum as a young woman.

Captions for the photographs follow the same order that the pictures were placed in the original photo album.

Samuel Weist

Samuel M. Wiest (1819–1866) married Ester Hette Baum (1820–1910). He is the father of Tobias B. Wiest, Mary Ann Baum's father-in-law.

George Baum

George could be the brother of Mary Ann Baum. This is the second picture in the album, which appears to be in chronological order. Therefore, older generations precede younger generations.

A newspaper clipping shows "the late George Baum of Herndon" standing in front of the parsonage in Urban in 1890. George is pictured in the photo with a fancy enclosed carriage drawn by two horses used to pull a casket. Mr. George Baum, the middle-aged undertaker in the photo, would be of the appropriate age in 1890 to be Mary Ann's brother. George may be a younger brother of Mary Ann.

Emma Wiest
Daughter of Tobias and Mary Ann, married Jacob Dimmler and lived in Fountain Springs, close to Ashland. Jacob worked at the railroad yard in Gordon.

John B. Wiest
He is the oldest son of Tobias and Mary Ann Wiest.

Monroe B. Wiest

1885–1970 He is the youngest son of Tobias and Mary Ann Wiest. Anspach
photo, 1895, copy by J.A. Romberger, 2007.

The Williard Girls
Barbara, Ellen, and Catherine with their mother, Ellen Jane
Genealogy of Johan Peter Williard, p. 24, by Wendy L. (Williard) Martz. The Harrison
Williard family resided in Lykens Township, Dauphin County, in the area known as "Spain."
The Bryant Troutman family presently owns this farm. Harrison Williard, (September 13,
1850–February 27, 1917). He was born in Hebe and died in Dauphin County. Harrison
married Ellen Jane Snyder (1850–27 Mar. 1920). She died in Dauphin County. Children
include Samuel Morris (b. 1876. Morris lived at the current residence of Terry and Maria
Williard, west of Klingerstown), Barbara (b. 1877), Ellen (b. 1878), Catherine (b. 1879),
William, Franklin (b. 1885), Isaiah (b. 1888), and Perry (b. 1891).

John Geise

John and Emma S. Geise, circa 1888. John was a carpenter. He is known to
have built his own home. This dwelling was later the residence of Allen and May
Rothermel. Tim Landis, the last resident, removed the dwelling and built a new
house. John also built the home for this author's grandparents, the Stanley and
Verna Romberger homestead, now the residence of Clay Shadle.

Miss Jennie Wiest

This young lady must be the daughter of John B. Wiest. She married Jacob Maurer, pictured later in this album. There is another person of the same name described below.

Sarah Jennie Snyder (1875–1950), daughter of Peter Snyder, married Samuel Baum Wiest (1878–1957). This Samuel B. Wiest is "Butcher Sam" Wiest. "Butcher Sam" is the brother of Tobias Wiest.

Samuel Clark

Samuel Clark Jr. and Johanna (Wiest) Clark were storekeepers in Klingerstown from 1885 to the early 1900s. They had a daughter, Elmira (Clark) Romberger, who married Isaiah Romberger. Samuel is the son of Samuel Clark Sr. Johanna is the daughter of Moses (Merkel) Wiest and Maria (Schadel) Wiest. Johanna was one of eight children (reared at Klingerstown Mill). These people were early pioneers in Klingerstown. Information from *The Klingerstown Bi-Centennial Album*, page 244.

Richard Wiest

Richard Wiest (July 9, 1855 – March 13, 1877) is the son of Samuel M. Wiest and Ester (Hette) Baum. He was a younger brother of Tobias Wiest. Richard and Tobias were born on the Eugene Erdman farm. This photo shows an older boy in a cap. Richard is included again, later in the album, as a young man.

Homer Cooker
Infant in dress, seated.

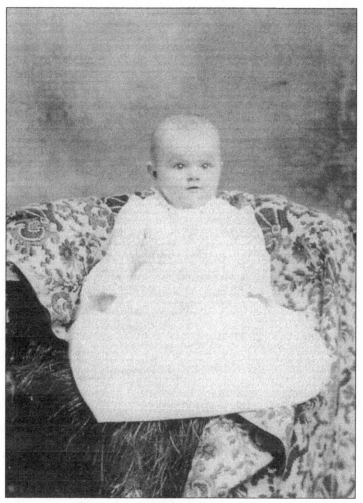

Roberta Eiley
Tiny infant in dress.

Sheffer Family
Sheffer may be the same common name of Shiffer. Photo by J. C. Williams, Reynoldsville.

Charlie Bixler
A well-dressed youngster with a fancy bow tie. Photo by Kehrwieder, 17 Independence St., Shamokin.

The Children of Victor Wiest

Victor Wiest was a storekeeper in Klingerstown. His son, Brian Barr Wiest, was a Wiest historian. Brian operated the Hollywood Movie Theater in Elizabethville. He is buried in Klingerstown at St. Michael's Cemetery.

Welsy, the baby

Appears to accompany the previous picture of the Victor Wiest children. Photo omitted.

Katie Williard
Ripple Photography was in Sunbury. Daughter of Harrison and Ellen Jane (Snyder) Williard. See the previous photo of the Williard girls.

Emma Wiest
Emma is the oldest daughter of Tobias and Mary Ann. See the previous photo.

Billy Bowman and Family

William Bowman was referred to as "Billy" by family and friends. Communication with Randy Bowman of Klingerstown confirms that Billy was his father (Casey's) grandfather. Billy was the undertaker in Pillow.

Richard Wiest

Richard Wiest as a young man. See the previous photo caption of Richard as an older boy in a cap.

John B. Wiest

A well-dressed young man with a big bow tie, wearing a vest with a gold watch chain. He is the son of Tobias and Mary Ann Wiest. John married Sevilla (Wiest) Wiest. They lived in Portland, Oregon.

Kitty and Lola Wiest
Appear to be the children of Victor Wiest, by comparison to the previous photo of the Children of Victor Wiest.

Mary Ann Wiest
Picture signed by Mary Ann Baum Wiest Annspach photo from Pillow.

Ella Wiest

Ella Wiest was born about 1885. Ella married Harry Schade. Harry was born about 1885. They resided in Alberta, Canada. They had the following children between 1905 to 1913: Ralph, Clarence, Tillie, Nellie, Gertrude, Burle, Charles, Burt, and Rebecca.

Jacob Maurer

Jacob D. Maurer is the son of Charles Maurer. Charles is the son of Daniel M. Maurer, who resided in Rough and Ready on the Henry and Wanda Reiner farm. Jacob D. Maurer married Jennie Wiest. They had 16 children. Jennie Wiest was the daughter of John B. Wiest. John Baum Wiest succeeded to his father's farms in Jordan Township but sold them to his nephew "Butcher Sam" Wiest. John B. Wiest then moved to Lethbridge, Alberta, Canada, eventually returning home to Klingerstown. Maurer Family history is recorded in *Tulpehocken Trail Traces*, p. 115, by Steve E. and Joan E. Troutman.

Charles Wiest
Edward Troutman Wiest (1854–1927) married first Catherine Musser (b. 1854), second Edith Musser (b. 1860). Edward's son Charles was born in 1873 in Malta, Northumberland County. He worked as a fireman on the railroad. Edward T. Wiest was born on what is lately known as the George and Mary Troutman farm.

Leo Troutman
Leo was born on October 9, 1905, the first-born child of Sally B. Wiest and Victor
W. Troutman (photo courtesy of John A. Romberger).

Jacob Klinger [Mary (Rabuck) Troutman Photo Collection]

Mr. and Mrs. Charles Heckler family, left to right: John Klinger, William Rabuck, son of Anson and Sarah Rabuck, Mrs. Mary Heckler, wife of Charles, Mr. Charles Heckler, Mrs. Jane Deibert, Sarah Rabuck, Kate (Klinger) Rabuck, wife of Theodore. Baby unknown.

Log home on the Troutman Brother's farm in Klingerstown, (1) Baum (2) Wiest (3) Troutman {Sally Troutman Photo Collection).

The log home of Victor and Sally (Wiest) Troutman.

John and Ada (Klinger) Troutman home, mid-winter scene. This double residence is the home of Allen Troutman and Michael S. Troutman.

George L. Troutman at the home of Victor and Sally in Klingerstown.

A reunion of Wiests in Jordan Township on the George and Mary Troutman farm, the early 1900s.

All in the family, *left to right*: Leo Troutman, George Troutman, John Troutman, Howard Williard, Victor Troutman, Jacob Dimmler.

Sally (Wiest) Troutman (1882–1972). A birthday party for Sally, possibly in 1967, when she would have been 85 years old. Standing left to right: Harry and Amelia Troutman, Katie and Leo Troutman, Mrs. Howard (Mary) Williard, Monroe Wiest, (died in 1970), Ada and John Troutman, Mrs. George (Mary) Troutman, Mrs. Guy (Blanche) Troutman, and Mrs. Johnny (Juno) Troutman. Front row: Ray Troutman, Sally Troutman, Guy Troutman, George Troutman.

The old Baum/Wiest farm was earlier divided and is presently the residences of Troutmans and Williards. Troutman Brothers is located on the south and Michaels Foods is located on the north.

Two old Rothermel farms. Presently the Landis Farm (center) and Erdman Farm (right).

George and Mary Troutman Farm (center), Eugene Erdman family farm (right). Both farms were earlier in the Wiest family.

The residence of Valerie, Timothy, Emma, and Leah Specht (center); on the hill above is the George and Mary Troutman farm. The chain of ownership includes, Harter, Eyster, Wiest, and Troutman.

Jordan Township, Northumberland County, PA. Specht, Troutman, Landis, Erdman, and Richard L. Troutman. The farm of Richard L. Troutman was lately known as the Pit Hoffman farm (lower right).

Ira (Pit) and Florence Hoffman lived on this farm for many years. John K. Romberger and Alice (Troutman) Romberger owned this farm previously. John A. Romberger was born here in 1925. Richard L. Troutman is the owner in 2020.

About the Authors

Steve and Joan have been an item for a long time. They attended Line Mountain High School where they became friends before graduation in 1970. Steve and Joan were quite fortunate in the respect that they both had the opportunity to attend college, which was uncommon at that time. They were some of the first of their families to do so. Steve is a graduate of Franklin and Marshall College, and Joan, an alumnus of Susquehanna University. They married in 1975 and moved to Rough and Ready. Their home location was approximately half way between their parents' residences. They still remain in this location in Rough and Ready after 45 years. They consider it fortunate to be able to reside in the valley that they grew up in. Their children, Michael and Valerie live nearby, as well as extended family and neighbors.

This history book is mostly about Steve's relatives, however, this book would not be possible if it were not for Joan's computer skills. She is Steve's typist and manuscript advisor.

Steve and Joan have authored several family and local history books. They enjoy family reunions and like to promote local historical education. Their two granddaughters, Emma, 11, and Leah, 9, live nearby, give their lives purpose and their presence encourages Steve and Joan to pass on to others of the next generation a knowledge of their heritage found here in the Mahantongo Valley.

Made in the USA
Monee, IL
23 January 2022

89688077R00111